11/14

D1371597

Tapping the Wisdom
That Surrounds You

Tapping the
Wisdom
That Surrounds
You

Mentorship and Women

Elizabeth Ghaffari

 PRAEGER

AN IMPRINT OF ABC-CLIO, LLC
Santa Barbara, California • Denver, Colorado • Oxford, England

Library of Congress Cataloging-in-Publication Data

Ghaffari, Elizabeth.
 Tapping the wisdom that surrounds you : mentorship and women / Elizabeth
Ghaffari.
       pages cm
    ISBN 978-1-4408-3261-1 (hardback) — ISBN 978-1-4408-3262-8 (ebook)
 1. Women—Counseling of.   2. Mentoring.   3. Personal coaching.   I. Title.
    HQ1206.G495 2014
    362.83—dc23   2014020228

ISBN: 978-1-4408-3261-1
EISBN: 978-1-4408-3262-8

18 17 16 15 14   1 2 3 4 5

This book is also available on the World Wide Web as an eBook.
Visit www.abc-clio.com for details.

Praeger
An Imprint of ABC-CLIO, LLC

ABC-CLIO, LLC
130 Cremona Drive, P.O. Box 1911
Santa Barbara, California 93116-1911

This book is printed on acid-free paper ∞

Manufactured in the United States of America

To my mentors, my family, and friends,
who made these stories possible

Contents

Preface

Women often say they wish they could find a mentor. What exactly do they mean?

- A trusted friend, counselor, or teacher
- A more experienced person with whom they might be paired or matched
- Someone who could serve as an example as they advance
- Someone who might advise them in their careers, their education, or their networks

Women are searching for many different things: trust, experience, a match, an example, and advice. They want an advocate as well as a guardian angel or protector. They do not trust very many people within the business setting for several reasons: they are not familiar with it; they may not be comfortable with competition or risk; or they may face undesirable (even predatory) behavior.

They would like a friend and colleague with whom they could discuss things in confidence, a match for their skills or interests. They want someone who is already a leader—someone who is more accomplished and whom they might emulate. Above all, women seek someone who could show them the ropes, give them the answers, and explain the trials they will encounter on their journey.

The expectations are great—perhaps mythic in scale. So, who better to turn to for advice than Homer, who wrote *The Odyssey*—the greatest story and perhaps the origin of the term "mentor."

THE ANCIENT STORY OF MENTOR

The Greek tale of *The Odyssey* by Homer begins by reference to the earlier story of *The Iliad* when, 20 years before, Odysseus left his home in Ithaca to go off to the Trojan Wars, leaving his wife, Penelope, and his father, Laertes, in charge of his castle and domain. Odysseus asked his old and trusted friend, Mentor, to care for his newborn son, Telemachus. When the tale of *The Odyssey* begins, it is 10 years since anyone has heard of Odysseus's fate; suitors are now ravaging his estate and wooing Penelope, who has not lost faith that her husband will return. Mentor tries to kick the suitors out, but they ridicule him, Penelope, and Telemachus. The suitors don't believe Telemachus has the gumption to go seek his father, suggesting he is more likely to stay where he is until someone comes and tells him what to do.

Telemachus is depressed by the situation, fearing that his mighty father might not return and doubting that he could protect the estate and his mother from the drunken, thieving miscreants. He prays to the gods for help. Zeus, his daughter Athena, and Poseidon decide it is time for Odysseus to return home. Athena appears before Telemachus in the guise of Mentor, informing the son that his father is alive, well, and will return. She, through Mentor, tells him to man up, get out of his funk, and kick the suitors out.

Telemachus tries but collapses in tears—affirming that he is not quite ready for a challenge of that scale. He blames others rather than accept his own failings. On the advice of Athena, Telemachus begins preparing for a journey across the seas with some friends to search for news of his father.

Telemachus' journey takes him to Pylos and Sparta, where he is treated as an adult by good people and finally hears the news that Odysseus is alive and well. With newfound confidence, Telemachus heads home and meets Odysseus, who also has returned to Ithaca, disguised by Athena as a decrepit beggar to confuse and deceive the suitors. Father and son now collaborate to take on the drunken suitors. Penelope announces a contest to select a successful suitor: she brings Odysseus's great bow for a marksman contest. Telemachus persuades the suitors to put their weapons into the storage area. The suitors are so drunk they can't even string the bow, but Odysseus and Telemachus, together with other friends, rise up and kill the suitors. Telemachus then shows new maturity from his travels and experiences. He identifies the innocent among them whom Odysseus should spare, demonstrating a new sense of valor.

TAPPING THE WISDOM THAT SURROUNDS YOU

There are mentors all around us, ready and capable of inspiring and informing us if only we are aware of their presence and their lessons. When the computer industry was in its infancy, individuals interested in learning about how things worked would search out user groups where advanced and experienced programmers or hardware professionals gathered together to share questions and answers, and newcomers to technology would come to listen and learn. That is a modern example of effective mentorship.

It was a mentor-protégé relationship without the expectations or constructs of modern match-making, pairing, or dependencies. It successfully transferred knowledge. It provided the framework for new participants to learn, to bring fresh ideas to the more experienced members of the business community, and to create symbiotic relationships where small teams of colleagues could develop new computer-based solutions to complex problems. An essential prerequisite was that those who wished to learn prepared themselves and sought the lessons of those who came before.

Women can listen to and learn from the lessons of other women role models who surround them. They can select the wisdom that they need from the host of talent touching their lives throughout their early years, their education, their careers, their work and play. Outstanding mentors are everywhere. They probably are not likely, today, to stop and protect, coach, counsel, advise, educate, or pamper the young women protégés. They can't tend to the needs of young women without great sacrifice themselves. They barely have time to hone their own skills. They are busy doing all the things that are crucial and essential to their lives and professions.

The protégés of today have to catch their inspiration along the way. They have to take their skill and talent and make it worthy of attention. They have to do the selection, match-making, example-setting, idea development, and other facets of mentoring by tapping into the wisdom they find in the marketplace.

Mentors closest to us are often the most overlooked. They include our mothers, sisters, brothers, and fathers—all of the people who define home for us. Other mentors can be found in our early childhood educational experiences and throughout our learning careers and at play. We experience mentors at our workplaces. We can read the advice of a host of mentors in the media and learn from role models on the political stage. And we treasure the lessons of mentors lost—looking back in fond memory at the gifts they provided.

There are three types of stories in the pages that follow. Some are tales taken from the real experiences of friends and family. Other stories are about role models—women who mentor by the exemplary lives they have lived. The third type includes essays capturing the wisdom of specific mentorship lessons while searching for the meaning beneath. There are parallels to the story of Telemachus: how he encountered specific experiences, how he connected with admirable people, and finally, how he incorporated those lessons into his own life.

These are examples of tapping the wisdom of all the people who surround us with the hope that we might journey on the seas of uncertainty and return with great maturity and confidence to face the challenges as we must.

Acknowledgments

Mentorship is all about acknowledgements—thanking the people who have helped us in our personal and professional journeys. Recognizing those large and small contributions to our growth is an affirmation of the lessons learned.

These stories are the expression of thanks by many to many: family members, teachers, friends, role models, inspirers, and challengers. Once we start thinking about intentional or accidental experiences with mentorship, we become attuned to discovering even more stories and the lessons they provide us.

My special acknowledgements go to the women of achievement who have allowed me to present their stories in my books, *Outstanding in Their Field: How Women Corporate Directors Succeed* (Praeger: 2009) and *Women Leaders at Work: Untold Tales of Women Achieving Their Ambitions* (Apress: 2011). Their incredible generosity of time and inspiration were truly gifts to this author, but more so to all the young women of ambition who read and followed their advice.

The women in these chapters who gave their permission and support to the retelling of their personal tales and stories from their books, their lives, and their memories have earned my special thanks for their unique focus on different aspects of the mentor-protégé relationship. Likewise, the women who wrote their own stories of mentorship (Nancy Crovetti, Marilyn Guarino, and Frances Anderton) added personality and character to this collection.

My family, especially my husband, who read through rough early drafts provided the critiques only possible from dear ones, have earned my sincerest thanks for their help. I alone am responsible for any oversights or errors.

I am sincerely grateful to my editor, Hilary Claggett, who managed this project from beginning through the tortuous waters of book proposal reviews, first drafts, edits, typos, cuts and pastes, cover, and marketing of the end product you hold in your hand. My sincere appreciation also goes to Nicholle Lutz and the copyedit support team for their diligence and care. We are fortunate to have editors and publishers who continue to work with us to refine and redefine the manuscript in an era when it is almost too easy to toss out words on the screen and hope for the best.

ONE

At Home: Family Mentors

From the very beginning of our lives, our mentors, first and foremost, are the family members who coach and guide us to become the people we would be. Sometimes they tell us exactly what we want to hear. Other times, they tell us what we need to hear but wish we did not have to hear. Their words of wisdom stay with us almost forever.

The most obvious mentors at home include mothers (especially) and sisters. They can stretch our world. They can be the first recipients of our own early mentoring efforts—successfully or otherwise. Fathers and brothers also serve as the teachers we need to help prepare us for the challenges of our adult journey. Whether our family relationships are healthy or not, we can learn from all of them.

Caretakers come into our lives and bring their diverse experiences to augment our young, cloistered existence. They are among the first mentors to open our eyes and minds to the world of possibilities we might encounter. They teach us to dare.

Vacations offer unique mentoring and teaching experiences. Family members use their time together to construct new worlds seemingly out of nothing.

New households get created through marriage, creating opportunities for extended family members to become mentors and allowing us to tap their extensive experiences.

A spouse can be a partner and mentor, capable of providing solace during difficult times and pushing us out of our comfort zone into accepting new challenges.

READING AT NAP TIME

Angel's earliest memories of her mother are that she was always reading to her. When the big kids, Angel's older brother and sister, had gone away to school, she remembered her mother reading to her at nap time. At the beginning were the simple Golden Book stories: *Goldilocks*, *The Three Little Pigs*, and *The Little Engine That Could*.

Later, there were the tales of *Winnie the Pooh* and the poems for Christopher Robin (which Angel can recite by heart today). There were the *Tales of King Arthur and the Knights of the Round Table*, *One Hundred and One Great Poems*, *Br'er Bear* and *Br'er Rabbit*.

Her mother had a beautiful, lilting voice, soft and soothing. She could imitate Br'er Bear with the best of Disney's voice-overs. Hers was the perfect voice to send a little girl off to sleep. It was also the voice that brought the Knights of the Round Table right into the bedroom, talking of honor, glory, and challenges.

At the end, years of cigarette smoking took their toll on her mother's larynx and lungs. As her mother was preparing for the surgery that would remove all of the larynx and some of the lung, Angel remembered her mother sitting in her rocking chair, reading large historical novels the family had retrieved from the town library.

Lesson: The ability to share stories gives both peace and joy, even—or perhaps especially—in the face of great personal challenge.

IF YOU WANT TO PLAY WITH THE BIG BOYS, YOU HAVE TO BE PREPARED

The irony of this sage business advice ("If you want to play with the big boys, you have to be prepared—to play the game, to play rough, to get bumped around a bit") is that it came from a woman: Becca's mother. Not that she was advocating that Becca become an Amazon. That wasn't her style. Becca's mother was a tiny lady with the soft voice of reason. Becca's siblings passed her mother in height (barely 5 foot 2 inches tall) by their early teen years. It wasn't her physical stature so much as her emotional stature.

Becca's mother was a peacemaker, a soft-spoken moralist in an otherwise unfair, brutal, and challenging world. Isn't that what mothers do?

So, why would she say such a thing? "If you *want to play* with the *big boys*, then you have to *be prepared*."

Usually, this advice would be delivered in response to one of the girls' pleading (or more likely, whining): "Make them [the boys, Becca's brothers] play nice with us," or "Make them let us play [baseball, tennis, football, tag . . . whatever] with them." Becca's mother saw her job differently—not to "make" the world different for Becca and her sister, but to teach them what they needed to know in order to take on the world as they found it and to prevail.

Becca said she wasn't exactly the boldest, most courageous of children. She didn't adjust to nursery school or kindergarten as well as others. Maybe it was the confusion of being the younger child among what she remembered as constantly feuding older siblings. Not the best role models for how to get a "Satisfactory" rating in the Plays Well with Others report card column.

When Becca was supposed to start the first grade, her mother would walk her to the Pleasant Street School, pushing the stroller holding Becca's recently arrived little sister. At first, mother and daughter would walk all the way to the sidewalk in front of schoolhouse door. Then, little by little, Becca's mother would stop slightly farther back and tell her, "Okay, you can go on by yourself, now."

Maybe it was the uncertainty of the ever-increasing terrain that she was asking Becca to overcome. Maybe it was some deep-seated jealously of her new little sister, who would return to the safety of story-telling or the excitement of other games at home, while Becca had to face her first grade demons. Becca reached a breaking point when the path that she would have to follow to school appeared longer and more uncertain than the clear, straight shot back home. Becca cried, begging her mother not to make her go on alone. It would have been so much better simply to go back to the easy little-girl life of Becca's past and her little sister's present. Her mother talked to Becca there on the corner—as she always did at other crucial junctures in her life, whether she was there with her physically, as she was that day, or whether she was only in Becca's memories, as now.

"Do you want to go to school and see all the interesting things they're doing today? Do you want to play with all your friends? Do you want to make new friends and learn new things? We've walked this same path for days, now. You know this street and the next street, and then there's the nice lady with the stop sign who will help you cross Main Street to go to the school. You know how to do this, don't you? Sure, you can do this. I'll be right here waving at you."

And as scared as Becca was then, as huge a challenge as that appeared to be, her mother helped her affirm to herself that there were experiences out there that Becca really wanted. There was a big, interesting world waiting for Becca. Sometimes, that big world might seem scary and uncertain, but her mother was preparing her to be able to face the uncertainty. If Becca really wanted to do something, then she had to want to participate in that rough and tumble world more than simply stare at it, in fear, from a distance.

Lesson: If we truly desire something enough, then we will take the steps necessary to gain it. Nobody can do it for us—especially those who care deeply about us. The alternative to taking those steps forward is to stand and stare at a goal somewhere in the distance.

KEEP AWAY

When Vivien's younger sister was born, the difference in their ages was too small for there to be a major change in her life due to the new arrival. Vivien was seven years old when the youngest sister was born. Vivien was just able to feel, if not understand, the excitement that was bubbling in the household as the day approached for her mother and newborn sister to come home from the hospital.

They would be returning in the family's big black '48 Lincoln with the great big running board on each side. While the car's overall appearance was somewhat suggestive of a hearse, it was one of the few vehicles that could accommodate a large family. On that day, the Lincoln rolled up the winding driveway that encircled their great house and stopped near the garage at the rear.

As usual, chaos reigned as the children who were old enough to be party to this event tried to stand on the running board and look into the car to see the new baby. Being the smallest at that time, Vivien couldn't see anything at all through the window. She gave up, stepped away from the car, and pouted in frustration.

This was an invitation to Vivien's older brother to taunt her. He grabbed the baseball cap, which Vivien had begun wearing every waking moment, and tossed it to the other older brother, announcing the start of a new episode of that classic family game "Keep Away!"

Sucker that she was, Vivien tried to retrieve the hat, first from one boy and then from the other. Resistance was futile. Only when their attentions were diverted by their mother and baby sister exiting the car did one of them give a final heave of the cap way over Ol' Puddin' Rock into the larch trees and bushes of the upper orchard.

Crying in frustration, Vivien went hunting for her precious cap, found it, and returned to the now vacant driveway. Everyone was gone. She was all alone with her cap.

Vivien decided then and there that she'd get even. She promised herself that she'd never treat her new baby sister like that. She'd never tease her like that. Never. That'd show them.

Lesson: Sometimes the lessons that mentors teach us are the lessons about how NOT to behave.

EMMA

When Sharon was just thirteen, her folks left the family and split for Arizona. It was only for a few weeks for treatment of her father's asthma, if she recalled correctly. Or maybe her parents really just needed a vacation from it all.

For weeks ahead of time, Sharon's mother hunted far and wide to find live-in care for the family troop during their absence. She found Emma Cannady—probably the only black female in the entire town of Northwood in suburban Pennsylvania, and certainly the only other woman capable of taking care of a brood of rambunctious kids ranging in ages from four to nineteen.

Emma was one of Sharon's first female role models because she was always opening her eyes and her mind. Emma talked about her days as a rebellious young girl in Philadelphia: about risk-taking. Emma and her friends would get into a car and go drive somewhere far afield just so they'd have to figure out their way back home again. They were just day trips, but to a little girl like Sharon with simple, predictable paths to and from school, home, and the playground, Emma's experiences were like grand expeditions.

As Emma stirred her magical spaghetti sauce concoction for supper, she would tell Sharon (who was white) about the history of the Civil War, Reconstruction, the Underground Railroad, and the early struggle for civil rights. That was in 1958—long before there was a movement and even before grade school history classes included most of the reality of the Civil War era. It took another decade before Sharon ever saw college texts catch up to Emma's simple truths.

Emma was far more than a grocery clerk at the local Food Mart—where Sharon's mother found her working. Emma was a registered nurse, having somehow worked her way through a nurses' training program. Sharon remembered her white uniforms, so neatly starched and ironed. While a very large woman, weight-wise, and barely five feet tall, Emma exuded a sense of power by drawing from some deep well of rock-solid self-esteem.

Her waist-length hair usually was tied up in a very tight bun at the back of her head. Her face was round, her features smooth, her bearing regal. She was gentle and kind but tough as nails. She commanded respect and earned it at the same time. How fortunate for Sharon that the very first African American person she would encounter in her life would have such a strong and proud sense of herself and her role in time.

Lesson: Because of Emma, Sharon says she has a tendency to view other women of color as likely to be cut of the same cloth—someone who can teach her, someone with inspiring life experiences that reach beyond Sharon's meager world, and someone with a steel core tested by both time and events. Seldom has Sharon been disappointed.

VIVE LA DIFFÉRENCE! VIVE LA DIVERSITÉ!

Four sisters born and raised in a small town all had the same pair of parents—he was a traditional Philadelphia lawyer, while she was a traditional housewife. All four sisters were afforded roughly the same education and opportunities.

Yet you could not find four more different females.

One spent almost all of her adult years in that same little town. For over two decades, she cared for an ill husband; then, after his death, she retired to a life of travel, exploration, and constant learning.

One is a home-based medical transcriptionist, condo-landlady, and book club organizer who plays and organizes a seniors' tennis tour. Of late, she now relishes the time spent baby-sitting her grandson.

One is a single mother, former elementary school computer lab technician, dog trainer, and school book contract administrator who, finally in her fifties, returned to pursue her bachelor's degree—online.

One is an emerging technologies consultant and corporate governance entrepreneur.

So, if four girls from the same family and upbringing can end up spread across the four corners of the United States, representing four uniquely different perspectives, value systems, and priorities, then how on earth could anyone reasonably suggest there could *possibly* be just One Woman's Agenda in this day and age—politically, economically, or socially?

Lesson: The challenge is not how to color women red or blue or black or white, but rather how to respect differences that exist, naturally, among us. What are the unique abilities of different people to thrive and excel at what they do best? How can we respect and learn from these differences?

THE ISLAND

When school was out and summer was well under way, Dana's entire family would pack everything into a gigantic Lincoln Town Car towing a trailer behind. They would drive from Connecticut up to the start of the lake country in the backwoods of Maine.

Their destination was a twenty-seven-acre island near Monmouth, just north of Lewiston, near Augusta. That's how you locate small towns in New England: mention towns of ever-increasing size, moving up from small cities to larger cities until, at last, one is recognized.

Dana's parents bought the island as a summer vacation destination and an investment: not just in real estate, but also in their children. This was in the 1950s, when polio was known to be contracted at large public concentrations such as beaches and lakeside resorts or recreation areas. The island in Maine was an investment in the family's long-term healthcare.

The family named the island after the kids: all five of them. They called the island EL-DA-MA-NI-MA, a fabrication of a Native American name for the island, built up from the first two initials of each sibling's name: Elena, Dana, Mark, Nicole, and Martin. Of course, the name was never officially recorded, so you'll probably never find anything like that today on Lake Cobbeesseecontee, which *was* the real Native American name of the lake on which the island was located.

What Dana remembers most about the island was that it was barren of normal human accoutrements. There was nothing there until the family members made something happen.

There was a beach but no diving board. When they wanted to learn how to dive, they walked out to the end of a string of rocks and dove into the exciting depths of four feet of water. Soon, even that wasn't enough, so their father and brothers scouted the environs until they discovered an even better beach with large diving rocks at even more challenging depths, maybe six to eight feet.

There was a main cabin but no electricity, no running water, and barely room for all of the family members. When it rained and all were crowded indoors together, it seemed as if everyone tripped all over each other.

Little by little, they added to their tiny, unadorned world. The first enhancements, in the early years, were kerosene lamps. One light per reader, another for the cook, and another big one for the dining table. Things seemed closer and gentler under the shaking soft glow of the lamp.

Later on, there arrived a gasoline-driven electric generator to power electric light. Dana never forgot—or forgave—the intrusion of the sound of that motor into their peaceful lives.

Water was brought up the hill every morning, bucket by bucket, carried by the currently responsible child. At first, the bigger boys, being much stronger, were given the daily water carrier chore. They would flaunt their strength, heaving over-filled buckets one on each arm.

Dana longed to hold just such a position of responsibility. To perform the water carrier ritual meant you had become "a big kid." Dana's older sister held a divergent view: she thought that all labor was menial and beneath her.

Their father recognized the different levels of strength that existed between girls and boys. He fashioned a wooden ladder made of beach tree branches. One bucket full of water would just fit between the middle rungs. Any two children of roughly the same height could team up to carry a bucket of water up the hill. It took some testing to make the journey and minimize splashing most of the water over the bucket edges. Dana and her sister learned to cooperate in order to avoid having to make two trips of half-full buckets before they grew enough in strength and stature to carry their own water individually.

Lesson: Making something out of nothing is an essential creative process. Not everyone views each opportunity as a positive, but teamwork can be taught.

THE MILK CARTS

Twice a week, during summers on a small island in New Jersey, a member of Theresa's family would take the twenty-minute boat ride from the island they owned to the mainland then walk a few miles up the rutted dirt road to the Ricker's Farmhouse, located on the main road into town. Waiting there would be a case of a dozen bottles of milk and other dairy sundries, which were left for pickup. This chore usually required two children to carry the case between them back down the road to the boat and over to the island. As the boys grew up, the chore reverted to the smaller girls, and the need for some assisting technology soon became obvious.

Theresa's father purchased an old, battered stagecoach from some citizen on the mainland. The wheels were easily four feet tall. He separated the stagecoach frame into two parts. Each half consisted of one pair of big wheels linked together by an axle, from which two great arms reached forward. In the vehicle's earlier life, these perpendicular arms had reached to the horses' shoulders or had connected the back axle, under the coach area, to the front axle. On top of each axle, their father built a box at the center to hold the milk case. One pair of wheels, thus redesigned as a cart, was parked on the island side, while the other was parked on the mainland side.

Now, two girls could go across to the mainland, take the cart up to the Ricker's Farmhouse, load the milk into the box, and, easy as you please, roll the cart back down and load up the boat waiting at the shore. On the island side, the process was reversed.

At either end of the errand, the giant wheels of the former stagecoach accomplished the objective of making it much easier to carry the milk crate. It also made the trip much faster, reducing the odds of heat spoiling the milk.

The cart that stayed on the island became another source of entertainment. Theresa and her siblings discovered that they could stand on the axle, straddling the wheel. Two kids (of roughly equal age and ability) would position themselves facing in opposite directions. At the count of three, each child would pull or push the wheel within his or her control and try to unseat the other, much as in log rolling. The perpendicular arms of the cart that extended forward from the axle provided a slight braking effect by dragging on the rough grass. It was just enough of a drag to allow the players to adjust their balance and prolong the game. The milk cart log-roll provided endless hours of entertainment and challenge during the summer months.

Lesson: Children, to grow properly, need opportunities to run, to jump, to carry their fair share of the burdens of life in a community, to test themselves by their own measures as well as others. But most of all, children need opportunities to learn the wonder of making something enjoyable out of nothing.

TEACH YOUR CHILDREN WELL

The late 1950s was the end of the big band era, but when a Big Band came to town, it was still an opportunity not to be missed. Tommy and Jimmy Dorsey were together with Gene Krupa at the Ambassador Hotel in Los Angeles, perhaps for their last tour. Tammy's parents couldn't miss it. Everyone was all dressed up, packed up, and loaded up into the car for the trek into "the big city" for a one-night, once-in-a-lifetime dinner and show.

The kids were awed by the red and gold velvet of the hotel. Everything at the dinner table was formal white and shining silver. Tammy's older brother, a waddling twelve-year-old, took a piece of paper, which their mother had rustled up from the depths of her huge purse, and he managed to get autographs from all the musicians. Today that would be a priceless piece of paper had anybody had the good sense to keep track of it.

The evening wound down. Everyone went to bed late. Tammy shared a room with her younger sister, Sarah (the baby). At ten years old, Tammy wasn't that much older.

The next morning, waking up before the sunrise, Sarah was wailing away. Whether from the late night hour of the prior evening, the drinking, or fatigue, it appeared that Tammy's parents could not hear the baby crying, nor did they respond to Tammy's prodding. It was just the two little girls wondering what to do.

Tammy was hungry and so thought that that must be Sarah's problem too. Tammy went to where her parents kept some pabulum and milk for the baby and started to make the mash before discovering there were no utensils to mix the ingredients together. Tammy remembered that, earlier, her father had called some store in the hotel called "Room Service," so she tried the same thing.

She dialed O for operator, asked for Room Service, and, when they responded, she imitated what she thought her father would say under the circumstances:

"May we please have a *spoon* for the baby's breakfast?" (just as her father had asked them for *milk* for the baby's meal).

Before too long, a young man dressed very much like the "Call for Philip Morris" bellhop came and knocked on the door. When Tammy opened the door, the man presented one shining silver spoon placed delicately on a white linen napkin covering a silver platter.

Tammy reached for the spoon, thanked him, and stepped back to close the door.

"Do you need anything else?" he asked ever so politely. "No thank you," she replied and thanked him again softly while closing the door.

Tammy finished preparing the pabulum and milk, tasted it herself, and wondered how babies ever tolerated the goop. It quieted Sarah down until adults could attend to the other, more serious business of diaper changing.

When Tammy told her father how she had managed to ring Room Service for a spoon for the baby, all he could ask was, "Did you give him a tip?"

"What's a tip?" she asked. Here she was, *so* proud of herself for being the responsible adult when nobody was around. And yet she *still* couldn't seem to get it right.

Lesson: Teach your children well. Teach them from the start to the ending. For whatever you do in your life, they will mimic your actions, follow your lead. If they don't know how to finish what they have begun, perhaps it is because you have not finished what you have started.

LOOK IT UP!

When Frances was young and just learning how to read and spell, her parents introduced her to the concept of how words come together by sounding out the pieces, or letters, of the word. It was like a puzzle that sometimes she solved and sometimes she did not—as in neighbor or weigh. How on earth do we learn English?

But once she made it past basic phonetics, Frances next learned the challenge of The Dictionary—that universal answer to the childhood question of "How do you spell. . .?"

The family didn't have just your ordinary Webster's Collegiate Dictionary with a couple of hundred pages. Oh, no—that was not good enough. Frances's folks had the dictionary that was two feet tall, over a foot wide, and a half foot deep. It was so huge it had its own wrought iron stand. The book sat there, spread eagle, open to the last challenge some sibling had solved—on or about page 5,761: scrophulariaceous to scutellum.

At the beginning of her school life, perhaps as early as first grade when first challenged by spelling tests, Frances learned The Universal Truth.

"If you don't know a word, you look it up."

"But if I don't even know how to spell the word, how am I supposed to *find* it in the dictionary?" she would try to argue. But her folks had heard the same excuse before and would reply with the inaugural challenge:

"What does it start with?"

Frances would be slowly guided forward from the starting letter, then the next one, and the next . . . testing with each subsequent letter to see if the dictionary and the investigator agreed that these two, then three, then four letters should come together to resolve the fundamental question of "How *do* you spell it?"

Frances learned that once you actually delve into searching the dictionary, funny things start to happen. On your way to discovering Ultimate Truth, you see other things that catch your eye.

Perhaps a previous search had left the dictionary open to W. On the splayed page, Frances would see pictures, diagrams, maybe even some tables.

"Hey, did you know they had a whole page on all the Weights and Measures?"

"Look at this diagram of a wheelbarrow from China. Amazing! And a windmill. Interesting!"

"Where was I? What was I looking for?"

Looking up words in the dictionary taught her more than just how to spell. It also taught her how words were created by combining ideas from our past to serve our present and future needs.

Take the word "technology." The dictionary says it's from the Greek: "*techne*," meaning "an art, a skill, a craft." Who would have thought it would *not* say "something Microsoft or IBM invented"? Not at all. It starts with an idea from centuries ago—from Greek origins—and it harks back to the most fundamental forms of human creativity: art, skill, craft.

There's also that other half of the word, "-logy" from the Greek word "*logos*." After all, this is how it all happens—putting two things together— *techne* and *logos*.

"Logos" means "word, thought, speech, discourse" and is a common suffix attached to other terms to convey the idea of "the study of" or "the field of." Examples are biology or physiology. What is "discourse?" Visiting the section starting with the letter D, she found "the act, power or faculty of thinking consecutively and logically; reasoning power, coherent reflection on thought."

So "technology" could be thought of as "the field or study of an art, skill, or craft." And in learning how to spell the word, Frances also learned how it was crafted. She traveled out of ignorance about how one spells "technology" through the origins of Greek thought, passing by weights and measures, wheelbarrows, and windmills, onto the study of "logos" and the discovery that "discourse" is much much more than merely words and speech.

Lesson: If we are simply told the answer to a question, we will miss the excitement of the discovery process. One word is not just a collection of letters—a word can span centuries and serve human creativity from the time of manual labor all the way through to the knowledge of today's economy, web domains, servers, and networks. Every word is worthy of the journey of "looking up."

LEARNING FROM OUR BROTHERS

Gloria has always learned a lot of things from her "brothers," which in-clude two real brothers, one terrific husband, a son, a whole slew of profes-sors, bosses (some better than others), peers, friends, even enemies—all of the male persuasion.

By substituting a view of peers in the office as brothers and sisters, Gloria learned how to increase the likelihood that the office environment served as a setting of individual achievement, of team members reaching their greatest potential by pursuing their own personal goals rather than looking at each other as sexual partners.

Looking at men in an organization as "brothers" is somewhat more respectful and egalitarian than the alternatives: potential dates, potential spouses, or daddy figures. A "brother" would do no harm to a "sister" in the best sense of the words.

Gloria's son provided another learning experience when he entered the Marine Corps and told her of their concept that "all Marines are green"—with no prejudice implied by gender, race, religion, skin color, or other visible or invisible indicators. All Marines have the same equal opportunity to excel. This is more egalitarian than even "all Marines are brothers."

Gloria read many stories from the early days of women becoming medical doctors, before women were allowed to enter medical schools, be certified by state medical boards, or to practice medicine. Pioneering woman like Margaret Floy Washburn and Elizabeth Blackwell benefited from the help of male colleagues, brothers, and uncles in their search to learn how to treat the women in their communities who were being essentially left untreated by male members of the established medical profession.

Gloria believed that women who want to succeed needed to learn how to emulate some of the behaviors of men, while also not *becoming* men, man-like, or male-like. Women want to retain their sense of themselves as females and to be comfortable as themselves—which they can be as a sister. This is different from a relationship with either potential dates/spouses or daddy figures—where women believe they have to change or conform to others' expectations. They can be themselves in a brother-sister relationship. Women can be themselves as sisters to their brothers.

The concept of learning from our brothers also implies that women can learn the rules of the corporate game from peers who understand them—in fact, from the peers who usually created all the rules of the game—brothers. Guys tend to create the rules of engagement in most environments, so it makes sense for sisters to recognize this and to get an understanding of how the rules work from those who made the rules—the brothers.

Lesson: In order for women to reach the top levels of success in any contemporary profession, they have much they can learn: investment strategies, rules of procedure, risk-taking, strategic planning, financial savvy, etc. Just as female doctors and lawyers learned the rules of those professions, so too can women acquire the expertise and competence associated with risk-taking, negotiations, financial leverage, and the economics of the marketplace. Where else are they going to learn all of this, if not from "their brothers" already at the top of the profession?

BABUSHKA

Safieh Rafatjah was born in Moscow on the 26th of June in 1903. Elizabeth knew Safieh because she married Safieh's nephew. Together, they published the story of Safieh's life in 1978. Safieh wrote it all down in her 75th year while pursuing a certificate of English proficiency from the British Council in Tehran, Iran.

One day in the late 1970s, Safieh had given Elizabeth a journal in which she had written essays about her life and times as a way of perfecting her grammar and writing style. Elizabeth had moved to Iran with her husband and first met Ame-jan Safieh in Berlin as they passed through Europe en route to Iran. "Ame-jan" is Persian for, literally, "dear sister of my father." Ame-jan Safieh was living with her daughter and her daughter's husband, an attaché from Iran to West Germany.

Safieh's journal told the stories of her life, how she was among the first women in medical school in Moscow, one of about three hundred students entering in 1925 and graduating in 1930.

Safieh did the unthinkable for an Iranian female of that era—she told her prospective husband that she would marry him only after she finished her studies at the medical college. He agreed.

She began her medical practice in a small hospital in Makhachkala, in South Russia, where her husband was assigned as an Iranian consular attaché. Next, they went to Tehran in 1932, Iraq in 1935, Baluchistan in India in 1936, and then returned to Iran in 1941.

There, she worked for the Iranian Health Department for twenty years. In 1961, she built a family-practice medical clinic with funds left to her by her brother. She was in charge of administration and finances until her retirement in 1970.

They had two children and endured the death of their only son. Her two grandchildren call her "Babushka" as a term of endearment for older Russian women. She worked through two major earthquakes—one in Tashkent and the other in Baluchistan. She outlived her husband, caring for him during his last years. She survived two revolutions—the Russian one at the beginning and the Iranian one at the end of the twentieth century.

She was a doctor when women were not supposed to go to medical school. She was an entrepreneur when women were not supposed to start medical clinics.

Safieh showed Elizabeth how to see the power and strength that lies just beneath the surface of what others might see as simple, unassuming women. Safieh's stories in her journal unfold quietly, gently, softly, and without pomp or circumstance, telling about her sisters and all of the other quiet yet quite incredible women in Elizabeth's husband's extended family.

Lesson: There are great women everywhere. Our challenge is to see the world through their eyes and to experience the world as they encountered it.

WHEN SOMETHING COLLAPSES

Irene and her husband arrived in London from the States at about 11:00 p.m. They fell asleep immediately upon arriving at the hotel, leaving a wakeup call for 5:00 a.m. the next morning. Pan Am flight #2 from London to Tehran had rescheduled an earlier-than-usual 8:30 a.m. departure in order to beat the curfew that had been in effect due to anti-Shah demonstrations in Iran in November 1978.

Pan Am said they were going to board passengers fifteen minutes early. At 8:15 a.m., they heard the last call for Pan Am #2 and nearly ran the full length of the terminal to the departure gate. As always, it was hurry-up-and-wait another ten minutes before, finally, they were told "first class passengers may now board."

Finally, when they were settled in, the inevitable happened.

"Small oil leak. Engine two. Please return to the transit lounge."

Six other jumbo jets were also delayed, jamming passengers and carry-ons into the lounge, shopping stalls, and coffee shops. The waiting seemed interminable.

Nine o'clock: ". . . should know by 9:30." Nine-thirty: ". . . should know one way or the other by 10:30." Ten-fifteen: ". . . repair underway, should be able to board by 11:00 a.m."

Twelve o'clock: still at departure lounge. One o'clock: ". . . cabin personnel prepare for take-off."

Irene is prone to exaggeration, but it does seem that every time she went on vacation, something happened back there in Tehran. It made her nervous about vacations. This time, it was much more unsettling to return. They first heard word of events when the hotel's UPI teletype spit it out:

". . .Three hundred seventy-seven killed by terrorist bomb in Abadan movie theatre." Then, a few days later: ". . . prime minister and cabinet changed." The next report said: ". . . thousands rioting on feast day, martial law imposed in eleven cities and the capital; thirty-seven killed." Then: ". . .ninety-seven persons dead" and ". . . public authorities report one hundred ninety-seven demonstrators dead; unsubstantiated estimates range in the thousands."

Irene had seen martial law before: in the curfews of Washington, D.C., and cities on the West Coast. She never liked riots. They always seemed to represent the collapse of something. She'd seen looting live and televised. The innocent were always the ones that lost. She'd seen bayoneted automatics at soldiers' shoulders, but the faces focusing down the marksman's line always seemed so young. Tehran in November 1978 was no different.

"Expected arrival time in Tehran will be 11:45 p.m. Once again, ladies and gentlemen, we are sorry for any inconvenience which our equipment difficulties may have caused you. Due to the curfew in Tehran, special arrangements have been made to take you to your destinations safely."

Touch-down, bus to terminal, passport check. Things seemed normal: the local airline's departure was 45 minutes after theirs, and of course, their baggage cleared first.

Outside the terminal, things were different. A small truckload of helmeted and armed guards moved in among the taxis, deposited two fresh troopers, and went away with the end-of-duty pair. The two new soldiers were as alert as the other four pairs dotting the front parking area of Mehrabad Airport's main terminal. Their eyes scanned the area for private vehicles. Irene's eyes locked onto the bayonet. Her mind jumped back to another blade that had threatened at a roadblock in Los Angeles, then jumped to a television screen depicting, too vividly, some Vietnam holocaust.

"Number fifty-two?" broke her trance. "Fifty-two *here*." "Number fifty-three? Fifty-three? Fifty-*four*!"

Busloads of people were leaving for hotels. The rest of the passengers were individually lined up to get a number that would provide access to one of the few taxis authorized to drive during the curfew. Irene and her husband were given ticket #125.

The number of taxis leaving well exceeded the slow progression of assigned numbers. Obviously, some natives had quietly cracked the system. Others had done it by paying off the controller to let passengers double up in the taxis.

Finally, "Number 125?" Suitcases thrown in, sit down, cross the driver's palm to leave *now*, before another piece of the mob could interrupt the quiet.

A hundred yards later, the driver turned out his lights and crept behind the other taxis leaving the terminal. Out of the near pitch darkness, a dozen figures moved quietly in and around the vehicles ahead. Moonlight reflected off the nearby chrome trim as they realized the extent of security imposed on the area.

Checkpoints one, two, and three were clustered together at each of the major connectors to the airport road. After Irene's taxi passed the third man- and machinery-laden van, theirs was the only vehicle traveling on the main arterial into town. It was a science fiction scene: so silent you could hear the hum of the streetlights above the purr of the engine.

Large trucks were parked at the main circle just on the edge of town. This checkpoint was different.

Irene's driver knew it, too: lights went out as he stopped about 100 yards from two sole figures on the edge of the street. One figure remained upright. The second moved into a crouch to look down the sight of the rifle. She could only see the circle of the rifle butt and his aiming eye. The driver slowly rolled down his window and extended his hand, which held papers encased in a plastic sheath.

A flashlight beamed on the driver's hand then moved up and down. The taxi advanced ever so slowly toward the flashlight, the car lights still out. As the driver's papers were checked, Irene could only stare at the automatic rifle now aimed directly at her from fewer than 20 feet away. Even the most inexperienced shooter could have hit his target from that position. A trained marksman, jarred into action by some uncertain movement on the passengers' part, would have had the same result. Her husband felt the anxiety, too, and clasped her hand. They both froze.

Irene looked at these two figures, barely children in uniform, wondering if they were more afraid than she. Wondering if a cough would scare them into action.

The inspection over, the flashlight passed them on. The armed guard, on signal, returned to a standing position as the taxi drove slowly by him. The automatic stayed in a semi-ready position.

All the fatigue of the four-hour delay and ten-hour flight was washed away by the nervous adrenalin that surged into their systems. They went through the same sequence with double guards five more times in the ten-mile trip home: desolate strips of city streets, the flashlight, the nose of the automatic rifle, the young marksmen, and then passage back to the abandoned highway. The only detectible variation was how quickly the guard went into his crouch. The driver, too, seemed to sense the change of tempo and stopped as soon as the gun was lowered into position.

Arriving safely at home, Irene could not shake from her mind the image of those young faces staring out from under the helmets and along the rigid sight-lines. She never knew if he ever lowered it completely: she never looked back.

Soon afterward, Irene and her husband returned to the States, essentially losing everything they had possessed in Iran. They found themselves staying with her brother-in-law until they could recover from the shock and loss.

Weeks later, they were sitting on the porch of her brother-in-law's home, looking at the peace and quiet of the backyard lawn. Her husband joined her, placing a yellow writing pad and pen in front of her. Then, he sat down at the patio table with his own pad and pen.

"Let's just try to brainstorm ideas about what we could do next, shall we?" he asked. And so they began anew.

Lesson: There are many disasters in our lives. It is all a matter of degree. Sometimes the best you can expect is to arrive home in one piece and be grateful for that. A mentor in such situations is one who pushes you out of your self-pity, away from the all-too-human tendency to focus on the loss, moving you instead toward the next page, the next chapter in your life.

TWO

At School: Educational and Childhood Mentors

Our journeys through schools afford us much more than simply the history lessons from books. Far more enlightening are the lessons from the human beings we encounter inside the classroom. Teachers inspire and guide us, grade us, discipline us, counsel us—all of which constitutes the concept of mentoring. Then, too, there are all of the other people we encounter at school.

Other students at school might show us what it looks like to think small. It may take a teacher as mentor to remind us how to think expansively, again. Life events have a way of intruding upon our lives and the way we want to be perceived by the world. Teachers, as mentors, might provide a buffer from the adversity of life events. Or strangers in distant towns will appear just when we need them and speak to us as if we were the adult decision-makers we wish to become.

Some of the richest experiences come from teachers who see in us potentials that we cannot yet imagine. They stretch us by expecting more of us than we thought imaginable. We respond to them because we so want to earn their respect and not disappoint.

Mothers and sisters continue to mentor us through life's early rejections. Then they hand us off to other adults at school who counsel and guide us by keeping expectations both high and attainable. Roommates, in high school or college, can be positive or negative mentors: friend or foe. Classmates will test us and teach us. Some will go on and become players on the larger stage of life. Researchers and academics, even outside of our own circle, will demonstrate how to solve real-world problems that we encounter in our experience. We learn their lessons by observing their success.

MRS. PACKARD

Mrs. Packard was Karen's first grade teacher, and she saved the little girl's butt. Mrs. Packard taught Karen that Not All Girls Think Alike.

Karen first encountered the power of "little girl cliques" at recess during the first semester of her first year of elementary school. One little girl looked and acted exactly like Margaret from the *Dennis the Menace* comic strip. Some girls come hardwired to intimidate, and Margaret was a perfect example.

Karen was not the most socially adept member of the playground set, so she was flattered when Margaret came and talked with her at recess.

Then, one day, Margaret asked Karen if she wanted to become a member of Margaret's religious faith. It doesn't matter which faith it was. All Karen remembers was that she liked the one she already had. Not that she was a religious zealot, mind you, because it's really hard to be a rabid Congregationalist. They sort of believe in leaving everyone to follow their own conscience anyway.

Karen remembers wondering, "Why would I want to change?" Margaret's mind was a lot more cunning. For her, a shared faith was a precondition to friendship. If Karen didn't want to convert to Margaret's faith, then Karen wasn't worthy of being her playground pal.

Karen replied, "No, thank you," and thought the matter ended. But a couple of days later, she was "brought up on charges." Margaret had told Mrs. Packard that Karen had slandered and demeaned her religious faith . . . in first grade terms, of course. Mrs. Packard was judge, counsel for the prosecution, and, thank heaven, she also turned out to be one great defense attorney.

"She doesn't like my religion," Margaret had told Mrs. Packard, adding that Karen should be held accountable for her civil tort. "Make her play nice with me," Margaret whined.

Karen showed abject confusion about the incident. Mrs. Packard must have read the total mystification on Karen's face and then asked some questions to probe for alternative versions of the incident. Mrs. Packard next began to test Margaret's intentions a little more deeply. Mrs. Packard may have been a first grade teacher, but she had years of experience with scores of Margarets on the playgrounds of life: she had pretty much seen it all before.

Mrs. Packard defused the situation with a few carefully selected words: "I'm sure there was no intention to harm your faith, Margaret. Everyone has a right to enjoy her own religious choice. I'm confident that was all she meant. Isn't that right?" she asked, encouraging Karen to mirror her, nodding.

Which Karen did like a dashboard bobble-head toy.

Karen never claimed to be the most socially savvy female on the playground, but that day she learned quickly from Mrs. Packard how to listen with almost a third ear to what the other little girls on the playground are asking her to say or do.

Lesson: Not all little girls think alike. When you need to prepare yourself to deal with all of the Margarets of the playground set, it's nice to have a Mrs. Packard on your side.

THE PATCH

When Wendy entered the second grade, her own library card proved to the world that she was an intelligent, responsible person entrusted with the community's most valued resources: its books. She could now choose the books that her mother and she would read at nap time or bedtime.

They began with the Orange Books, the biographies of great men and women. Then they graduated to the Blue Book series, with more complete biographies. What a wonderful world of so many great and creative contributors!

When Wendy wasn't satisfied that they had done justice to the most exciting part of a book, she would take a flashlight to bed at night and sneak an extra chapter under the sheets, petrified that her mother's warnings might come true: that she'd ruin her eyesight.

Wendy soon discovered that her eyesight was not all that perfect after all. She was pulled aside by the district nurse during the school's annual eye exam and was given a note to take home to her parents suggesting they send her to an ophthalmologist. That was serious stuff: like dentist trips, it meant an hour's train ride into "the big city."

It also meant glasses, but that wasn't the worst part. Wendy was told she had to wear an eye patch and do daily vision exercises to correct a wandering eye caused by weak muscles. While resistant to the rigors of the prescription, Wendy basically did what she was told to do, as embarrassing as it was for a second grade girl to wear an eye patch at school.

Mrs. Wheadon, her teacher, somehow knew exactly how Wendy felt and told her the patch would help her vision. But Wendy was too young to understand long-term benefits, so Mrs. Wheadon told her to think of herself as playing the role of Captain Kidd, as if it were part of a Halloween costume. Wendy took the part to heart, even telling her schoolmates that she might send them up the gang plank if they made fun of her. Probably more effective than those empty threats were Mrs. Wheadon's warnings to her schoolmates that she would schedule parental discussions with anyone who made fun of Wendy's situation.

Lesson: When facing an unknown challenge, sometimes it's best to imagine yourself dominating your circumstances. And it's always nice to have a co-conspirator who understands your situation.

IRMA T. JACKSON

Many can sympathize with being "the middle child." There were three older siblings in Linda's family, all of them with strong personalities. It seemed as if every teacher Linda had in school compared Linda to an older brother or sister whom they had taught in their classroom years earlier. On the opposite end of "the middle child" spectrum were Linda's two younger sisters, who benefited greatly from their parents' sheer exhaustion in the area of discipline. More accurately, the younger sisters got away with murder that would have earned Linda a spanking in her day.

So, she was greatly relieved when the family relocated to a small rural town just over the New Hampshire state border, where Linda could write her own academic story on a clean slate.

There she met Irma T. Jackson, the most tenured teacher at Pollard Elementary School. White-haired, stern, and strong, Mrs. Jackson had goals of her own yet to be attained. Linda became an unwitting party to her strategies. Mrs. Jackson decided that the seventh and eighth grade students should learn about leadership, so slates for class president, vice president, secretary, and treasurer were drafted by the faculty. Elections were held, and Linda was elected president. If anyone questioned how the new kid in town could stage such a come-from-unknown victory, nobody ever saw it hit headlines. The faculty pretty much controlled everything in those days.

Linda became the vessel into which Mrs. Jackson poured her leadership wine. She taught Linda how to run the lunchtime executive meetings—which consisted mostly of the treasurer's report of lunch money earnings during the past week and "Council's Plans" for the next class speaker. It was Mrs. Jackson who reached into her connections to identify executives from the community to speak and provide the students with real world advice: civics from *civitas*.

One all-class session that Linda remembers well was when the president of the local community bank spoke about how the students could build credit by saving money in a passbook savings account, how the bank would pay interest for the privilege of holding student money, and how that wealth accumulated into capital that could be tapped by everyone in the town who wanted to buy a home or expand a business. Heady stuff for a fourteen-year-old! Linda, being the leader she was, opened a savings account that very week, which probably was the bank's plan all along.

Imagine what it must have felt like—to have once been hidden in the middle of a crowd of six kids, and now there's your picture introducing the head of the community bank in the local newspaper. Even though the photo was located on some back page, it was still a president-to-president moment.

But Linda didn't feel the glamour as much as she felt the responsibility of meeting Mrs. Jackson's expectations, the challenge of keeping her young peers in tow, making sure they would not damage the reputation of the seventh grade class before other adult leaders, like the banker, or in joint sessions with the eighth grade class and its leaders.

Scary stuff, this governance thing. Certainly, as the 7th grade president, Linda was a marionette in the hands of Mrs. Jackson. Then Linda earned her badge for real when she was elected, on the merits, to a second term as 8th grade class president.

Lesson: Who knows what else this young woman dared to do later in her life, only because some wise woman in a small town in an out-of-the-way school district had a vision that she could teach civics in a far more interesting way if she could collaborate with this young, impressionable girl, struggling to find herself, her place, and her part on this strange new stage?

EXPECTATIONS

Meg always felt like a round peg trying to fit into a square slot. The change from sixth to seventh grade was pretty traumatic. In the sixth grade, there was one teacher, one classroom, and multiple subjects slotted nicely into neat, fifty-minute segments. In seventh grade, called junior high school, there were dozens of teachers, different ones every day. You had to make a mad dash to different classrooms and remember which subject was on which days. Madness.

Somehow, Meg made it through junior high school. But then there was the bigger threat of high school. The little town in which she lived was so small it couldn't afford its own high school, so all the students went to the regional high school. The really, really *big* regional high school. As bad as that might have appeared on the surface, the really really *really* big problem was the pregnancy rate of young girls there. Overhearing conversations between her mother and father created images from *West Side Story* or *American Graffiti*. The decision was made to find an all-girl's school for Meg.

So Meg's mother began the search. Meg's mother was a traditional stay-at-home mom. And this was 1960—decades before search engines existed. Somehow, the local library provided the catalogs and counsel that Meg's mother needed to develop a short list of possible private schools for her daughter.

Meg went through the interviews, all dressed up in the best dresses from her closet. But that wasn't enough for the women of the Academy. "She's not an Academy girl," they told Meg's mom. "She's just 'not like us.' Meg is a tomboy. She just wouldn't be happy here."

Rejection at fifteen years. Meg's mom didn't accept the inevitability of the regional high school alternative. So, back she went to the library career counseling section. She kept up the search and found a more distant school with a greater emphasis on academics and a wide variety of extracurricular activities. Meg applied and had a most pleasant interview— actually just a conversation—with a graduate of the school who happened to live two towns away. Meg was accepted, sight unseen, for both Meg and the school.

Meg and her mom spent the summer shopping for the school's required shoes, skirts of the acceptable length, and other necessities. Meg sewed her name tags into everything.

In September, Meg was ready for the three-plus-hour drive out to the far reaches of the state when a hurricane swept through their small New England town, tearing up trees, knocking down utility poles, and generally forcing everyone to stay at home until emergency vehicles could clear safe passageways. It was five days before the weather and roads cleared enough for Meg to join the other students who lived much closer to the school.

When Meg arrived at the school, she learned what it really meant to be different. The other girls knew everything she didn't. They knew every schedule: waking, classes, eating, studying, and sleeping. They knew where every class was located. They had spent a week learning the names of everyone in the dorms and every teacher. Everyone was a full week ahead of her.

Everything and everyone was new. The campus was spread across acres. Classes were in different buildings, dorms were on the edge of campus, the bookstore and the administration were at opposite ends. Meg's world had suddenly become gigantic.

At the end of the first term, Meg was struggling academically as much as socially. A counselor sent her a note through intercampus mail telling Meg she had "an appointment to discuss your grades." Meg wondered to herself why she hadn't just gone to the regional high school and gotten pregnant like all the others.

It took some time to find the counselor's office, but Meg kept the appointment as required. Ms. Walker welcomed her in and immediately tried to calm Meg down with familiar questions about home, the hurricane, how classes were going, and how Meg was adjusting. Ms. Walker didn't get in-depth answers to her queries, but she persisted anyway. She knew Meg was petrified and that this was unknown territory, but she just kept the conversation going.

Ms. Walker said, "I know you can do great work." Under the circumstances, Meg should expect there would be some period of adjustment to the new school, the counselor counseled. "Give it time. Come back and see me next month. We'll have another chat."

For the next four months, Meg met with Ms. Walker for a brief "chat" about classes, teachers, grades, and progress. Meg needed to hear that it mattered to someone that she could perform, that she could improve. Once she knew that this adult shared a belief in her, progress was the result. Everything else just seemed to fit into place.

Lesson: Expectations are like food and water to the starved soul. Once we nurture the mind, the bounty can be harvested.

ANOTHER ODYSSEY

Nicki was a sophomore in private high school, having left the protection of the freshman dorms and graduated to a single room on the main campus. In the first year that she'd been at Northfield School in Northfield, Massachusetts, she had not gone home for a weekend—as many other kids had done. She had even arranged to work at the school over the Thanksgiving holidays the first year and to work away from home over the summer.

It just wasn't pleasant at home—maybe too much drink, too much sibling strife, maybe just not enough interest. But sophomores are "wise fools," and so Nicki broached the possibility of taking a weekend home in the late fall, just as winter was coming.

She figured out the bus schedule that would take her from Greenfield, via Concord, back up north to Haverhill, where someone could (*please?*) pick her up and drive her home for the weekend. At the end of the weekend, the reverse bus trip would easily get her back to school, which had almost become a real home, in Northfield, Massachusetts. All her family had to do was simply let her off at the bus terminal in Haverhill, a mere 20 minutes away.

Nicki dared the weekend at home in hopes that—like all those times she'd been at home for visits by older brothers and sister—maybe she too could get "a chance to sleep late," or "a favorite meal," or some other token of being "the honored guest for the weekend." But sophomores really *are* "wise fools" after all.

So, Nicki went home for the weekend and found that other, more important things were going on and that people were busy and that maybe you could do this or do that, but don't get in the way of the really important work going on.

The weekend came and went, and soon it was time to drive to the bus terminal to catch the return trip to Greenfield. But the football game went into overtime, and the beer flowed heavy, as usual. Nicki started getting anxious, but it didn't make any difference. At almost the same time that the bus was scheduled to leave the Haverhill terminal, Nicki's father drove her from the house and raced futilely to an empty depot.

"Ah, but there's always the train," he said. So, he checked his personal Reading Railroad schedule then raced the car over to the Reading Station. "In thirty minutes, there's a train to White River Junction, Vermont," he said. "You switch there to another train to Northfield. Easy as pie." And he left to get back to the ball game.

Nicki loaded her bags onto the train full of skiers destined for White River Junction. It was a long ride halfway up the state of Vermont to catch a train coming back down, half the distance of the state of Vermont, just to go two-thirds the distance across the state of Massachusetts. Finally, the train arrived in White River Junction. Nicki asked the conductor, "Where's the train for Northfield?" He pointed to the one ahead. She got in and sat down among still more skiers, thinking, "I didn't know we had that big a ski team."

It was another long ride. And she dozed a bit here and there. The train stopped and everyone got out. It was dark at 11:40 p.m. The snow began to fall, ever so lightly. "So, where's the van to school?" Nicki asked herself. Never having taken the train from Northfield, she didn't have the slightest idea where to look or where to go. She saw a dimly lit sign over to the side, and thinking it would explain where YOU ARE HERE might be, she walked over and read, "Welcome to Northfield, Vermont, Home of Norwich University."

Northfield, *Vermont*? Where the hell is that? Where the hell is the ski team? Where the *hell* is anybody?

A nearby telephone booth was the only sign of civilization. Nicki looked in the Yellow Pages and called the first taxi cab company in the list. "How long a trip is it from here to Northfield, Massachusetts?" she asked. If ever there were a long, deep, sigh, it was right there on the other end of that phone.

"It's a pretty long trip—you're closer to Canada," explained the voice on the other end of the line. Nicki's stomach felt like it emptied itself on the cold snow-covered ground. "Is there a train out of here or a bus?" she asked, close to panic now. "Maybe you'd better come in out of the cold. I'll come and pick you up. We can talk over your options here at my house," he said.

Now she really panicked. Did she just call someone who's gonna kill her in this godforsaken place? Who would care at this point? In a while, the taxi came (at least it *looked* like a taxi), and what else was she going to do at this point? Seated in the backseat of the cab, Nicki tried to remember if she had any sharp objects in her purse, just in case.

He took her to his home. And his poor wife was there, staying up late to greet the pair with some cocoa. They talked about the options. The bus would be the next day. Can't rent a car because Nicki was too young, even if she could afford it. Couldn't afford his taxi rate, either. So—three hours of waiting to try it again to White River Junction. Another train, at about 2:30 a.m., could take her back to White River Junction, Vermont, then hopefully a better connection to Northfield, Massachusetts.

At least they were talking to Nicki as if she weren't the village idiot. They told her that this happened a lot more than anybody at school was willing to admit. Both ways—even the big guys at Norwich University were found lost, stolen, or strayed at the Northfield, Massachusetts station. (Now Nicki knew why the ski team was staring at her—Norwich was an all-boys campus!)

The cabbie and his wife were talking to her as the one who had to make the decisions. So, Nicki did. She opted for the train again—this time with a lot more information and depth of understanding about the consequence of a wrong choice.

At about 12:30 p.m., Nicki called her father and just gave him the facts— "I'm here, I'm doing this, and then I'm doing that. Good night." Next, she called the head of her dorm—who told her they'd have the security chief come pick her up in his squad car at the Northfield, Massachusetts, train station.

Nicki didn't sleep at all until it was time to go back to the Norwich University sign at about ten to 2:00 a.m. She switched from cocoa to coffee just to be alert for the big transition in White River Junction. The taxi driver waved to her as she boarded the train, reminding her to make sure she got on the train that was "the one in front"—the first one to go.

In White River Junction, now that Nicki knew what to look for, it was obvious that there were two train cars, one right in front of the other, both of which went to Northfield; the one in front went to Massachusetts, while the one in back waited and then went to Vermont.

She passed the long night alone with her thoughts, arriving in Massachusetts at about 5:30 a.m., where the squad car was waiting alone at the tiny station. Nicki fell asleep in the back seat as the security officer talked on, saying, "Sure happens a lot more than people let on."

Lesson: It is not really a problem of getting lost. The challenge is what you do when you have discovered that reality. Strangers can be mentors as much as friends.

CHECKS AND BALANCES*

Nina thought she might be one of the last people on earth to still get a paper statement from her bank. She'd sit down with the statement diligently, every month. She wouldn't spend another single cent until the last line on the paperwork matched the last line in her checkbook. It had been that way for the last forty years. Ever since one snowy weekend in Colorado, back in the seventies when her sister, Marilyn, came to visit, and Nina learned the art of checkbook reconciliation.

At the University of Denver, Nina was disinterested in money, banking, or finance. She was a free spirit theater major, "child of the universe," and admittedly advantaged. Her father paid her tuition and her rent. Naively, she thought money earned from summer jobs for incidentals counted as paying her own way.

During Marilyn's visit, a letter came from the bank: Nina was overdrawn. She thought it seemed more cautionary than threatening, but luckily for her, Marilyn—who had a background in economics—saw things differently. Nina could still see Marilyn, shaking her head in amazement and dismay, her eyes getting larger and larger as she scanned the evidence of Nina's financial ineptness.

"Okay," Marilyn said, taking a deep breath. "Are these all the statements? Do you balance your checkbook?"

---

*Written and contributed by Nancy Crovetti.

From the stacks of books and papers on her miniscule kitchen table, Nina unearthed a handful of bank envelopes—some unopened—beneath what she deemed more important: an essay on the history of women in dance. "Well," Nina answered lamely, "I try but. . .I just don't get it. . . ."

They both knew where this was going. Nina of the New Math was more than a little a numerically challenged: she was the poster child for Math Anxiety. When neither of her parents could help her with her fifth grade homework, she phoned girlfriends for answers, so she aced those assignments but then bombed the tests. Her very smart teacher figured it out and wrote a cautionary note on one of her tests: "You are only hurting yourself." Nina's mother was called in for a conference. The choices Nina faced were either to stay in from recess for help or to do extra practice problems at home. Part of Nina's problem was that she did not know how to explain what she didn't understand. It was a foreign language to her. That school year mercifully ended, and somehow she managed to squeak through another two years of upper elementary math. In high school, she proceeded to flunk Algebra I, Geometry, and Algebra II in succession, and had to repeat at least one semester of each. It all seemed inevitable—she was No Good at Math and that was that.

"Me balance a checkbook?" Nina heard the words, but nothing registered. Not only was it math, but also it was subtraction—terrifying in and of itself because it could only lead to smaller and smaller numbers. Nina would open the mailings, look through the maze of numbers, and then fold them back into their windowed envelopes, where they languished, hidden among the paper chaos of her kitchen table.

Nina's only experience with checks had been watching her mother work with an enormous checkbook register she kept for the apartment rentals she managed for her father. When envelopes stuffed full of cancelled checks came in the mail, her mother diligently would glue them back into the checkbook next to the receipts from which they had been torn. Those lessons proved useless to Nina, with her meager pad of checks and no bottle of LaPage glue. Nina thought that somehow she had missed crucial steps in the process of how to reconcile a balance.

"Okay," Marilyn said again. "Where's your checkbook?" She had started to open each envelope and methodically sort the paperwork by date. At nineteen years of age, Nina's idea of money management was to write checks for two dollars at the local pharmacy, just enough to buy a couple packs of cigarettes and have enough change left over for coffee at the diner with the theater crowd. She figured that if she only wrote *little* checks, then she wouldn't spend so much. Never mind that she ended up writing several "little ones" over the course of a week. Sometimes she would not record the check number or the date, so the register was a mess. There were at least three months' worth of checks and unbalanced balances to wade through.

Marilyn began with one stack of checks and one month's statement and showed Nina how to put the checks in numerical order then go down the list of checks on the statement and put a hash mark for each cashed check. Then they added up all of the checks not accounted for and subtracted them from the statement balance. It seemed doable: beginning balance, ending balance, and how they got there. They spent the rest of that afternoon figuring out the checking account for the past year. As it turned out, that letter had arrived just before Nina's father had sent a check—so while the balance was in jeopardy, she actually was in the black to the tune of about $10.00 after the overdraft fees. It was a close call, but real financial disaster had barely been averted.

To this very day, every month, without fail, Nina follows through on that lingering bit of mentoring and keeps her checkbook in balance—sans the $2.00 checks.

Lesson: There are no great words of wisdom to summon up from that afternoon, but there remains a lasting feeling of accomplishment, of her own capability finally realized and enduring. There was no lecture and no chastising: just sorting them out, lining them up, and checking them off. It was something she simply but absolutely needed to know how to do and needed to be taught.

MENTORING VISION*

Christie saw the world a little differently than her siblings did. She was born cross-eyed, a cruel twist of fate that made her the target of children's cruel taunts and imbued her with self-doubt at too young an age. Her earliest defenders and mentors were her older brothers and sisters, who fended off the ridiculers and helped her realize her own self-worth.

Corrective surgery at age six brought a newfound confidence. Christie recalls her third grade class picture—no longer was she the little blond girl with her head down, shying away from the camera. Suddenly, she was a cocky, ready-to-take-on-the-world child, luxuriating in being the butterfly, at last, instead of the moth. She flitted and floated all through elementary school in her new-found freedom.

---

*Written and contributed by Marilyn Guarino.

In their small rural town, where few would discover college or professional careers, a girl like Christie was destined to a dead-end life without vision. After the surgery, she now found herself in the center of the smartest, prettiest, and most socially accepted circle of girls and boys. Her older sister—a book worm, dean's list student, and student government leader destined for great things, saw a much larger world and provided Christie with a steady reminder that her lifestyle was too small, that she was swimming in a pond with no view to her future, and that—were she to remain there—her life would dead-end. Christie fought her sister tooth and nail. Unbeknownst to Christie, both her sister and her parents were conspiring on the matter of her future. So, off to private school she was shuffled.

A boarding school freshman torn out of her comfort zone and hours away from home, Christie was painfully unhappy. She could not see why she'd been torn from the life she loved and where, in her own mind, she was thriving. There she was, tossed into the midst of wealthy, urbane, and worldly young ladies, outcast because of her own self-absorbed sadness, homesick for the familiar, and completely miserable. Once again, she was the little crossed-eyed girl who just didn't fit in.

In time, Christie realized that mentors were determined to save her from herself and to help her realize her potential—despite her. Mentors were everywhere—the English professor who taught her to write persuasively with precision and direction, her caring housemother who encouraged her to express her feelings through her piano playing, her wonderful proctor who took Christie under her wing, choral directors and international piano teachers who taught her rigorous discipline and perfection that in her later years would guide her into a musical career of her own, student government leaders who set a crucial example for her in community organization and leadership. And always there was the endless support of Christie's older sister, holding her hand, taking her to lunch, letting her cry—but less and less with each passing day as she grew and began to see more clearly her pathway as it emerged and would lead her into a bigger world than she'd ever known existed.

Christie doesn't recall the exact day, but she does recall the moment, when she stopped and looked around herself, suddenly realizing that the veil had been lifted and that she could see. She was no longer the sad little crossed-eyed homesick child, but a young woman with a wider perspective and an understanding of where she'd been and what she'd become. Her many mentors had lifted her quietly upon their shoulders to a place of peace and clear vision. She could see what she needed to do.

And so, on the eve of her senior year, Christie applied for and became a freshman dorm proctor—and with that position, she became the mentor she once needed, holding onto the hands of many frightened young freshmen women, many from the ABC program—from underprivileged homes in Detroit, New York, and Chicago—who were desperately trying to adapt to a new world and culture they barely understood. She knew their pain. She encouraged them and cheered for them. She sat with them when they cried. She put her arms around them as her sister had done and supported them, joked with them, and told them she had walked in their shoes. Christie held the light up for them, shining it on their pathways, and promised them that even though their vision of the future wasn't always clear and that their eyes might not see perfectly what lay ahead, that eventually, with courage and with time, it would all come into focus for them—as it had for her.

Christie admits she doesn't dare think about where she would be without all of her mentors—probably a hausfrau in that small town tucked away in the mountains. But thanks to her mentors, she has become a capable citizen, leader, organizer, athlete, teacher, writer, pianist, singer, parent and grandparent. She pays attention to all the details. She promotes causes and programs. She is not afraid to stand up and tell everybody exactly what she sees—clearly, now.

Lesson: We may wish to stay in the comfort of our small pond until we are shown the greatness and power of our own potential in the eyes of those who care for us.

EYES ON FIRE

There was a time when Elise was convinced that she'd lost her sight. She was in graduate school and becoming just vain enough about her looks to wonder if contact lenses might improve things appreciably.

These were the days of hard plastic lenses that required gradually increased hours of usage per day over a period of six to eight weeks to allow the eyes to adjust. After about three weeks, Elise was up to a full ten-hour day, or so she thought.

She removed the lenses at dinner, finished supper and her studies, and went to bed. At about midnight, she woke up in a sweat with her eyes feeling as if they were on fire. She moved in the dark to the bathroom to splash some water on her face and eyes. When she turned on the light, it felt like a thousand tiny needles were piercing her eyeballs. She quickly turned off the light. The pain was so great, her lids refused to open again. She splashed cold water on her face again and held cold water in small pools against her eyelids with only temporary relief.

Slowly, Elise negotiated the hallway back to her bedroom, hand over hand against the wall. She lay back in bed with a cold wet face cloth providing almost no relief at all. She was convinced she was blind. The lenses must have severed something. Her life as she knew it was ended. In the morning, when her roommate Judy awoke, they'd have to go to the eye doctor. Meanwhile, Elise had nothing to do but feel sorry for herself, which she did intensely well—crying for at least half of the first hours of the morning. Pity, deep and heavy, weighed on her chest. She wanted to look at the clock, read a book, gaze at the stars, but each moment, each idea slammed her up against that same reality: *you can't do that anymore, you're blind now.*

As morning approached, Elise wondered, *what can blind people do?* Then she personalized it. "I'm intelligent, educated. What can I do? I'll have to learn how to read Braille. I wonder how long that would take. Where do they teach Braille?" Slowly, ever so slowly, her mind turned to the hunt for the next steps she'd have to take on this new turn in the road of her life.

At dawn, Judy, her roommate, awoke and tried to calm Elise back to reality. "We don't know what's wrong, yet. Let's take it one step at a time. No sense in planning your entire future until we know what we're dealing with. First, where's your eye doctor's phone number?"

Elise was deeply grateful to her roommate, in spite of the loss of freedom she felt. She had never felt so dependent on anyone in her life. The idea that Elise might have to rely on others to this degree for the rest of her life ate at her. Judy sensed the conflict and just kept at it, perfectly kind and patient, asking what Elise wanted her to do next and leaving as much control in Elise's hands as possible.

Elise still could not open her eyes. Judy drove to the doctor, who reported the pain and damage were temporary. The lenses were too tight for her eyes, causing an oxygen deficiency because there was no room for air circulation between the lens and the eyeball. Drops of liquid oxygen then and throughout the day, thanks to Judy's care, would slowly relieve the pain and gradually allow Elise to open her eyes again.

Lesson: Perhaps, if events dictate, we might have to test the trueness of our willingness to learn a new language, a new life, another way of relating to others and to the world. If that is the case, may we have good hands to guide us on that journey.

THE "NICE MEN" WHO TAKE CARE OF US

Dr. Alice Bourke Hayes, corporate board member and college president, once reminisced,

In the fifties, women were just not as career-oriented as they are today. In the back of our minds, we just assumed that some nice man would take care of us—a husband, a father, or a brother.[1]

In the 1960s, when Olga was preparing to choose a college, "the nice men" who would pay her way there assumed they had the right to select where she would go based on their criteria. Her father consulted with her brothers, and together they decided that Shelton College would position Olga well for the future that a young woman would face from 1964 forward. This all-women's college was equidistant from something like eleven dominantly or exclusively male colleges, thus dramatically improving the odds that she would find a husband who "would take care of her."

Olga's peers at Shelton apparently concurred whole-heartedly with that philosophy. While she foolishly attempted to focus her attention on studies, her roommate and dorm mates focused their energies instead on weekend dances and parties hosted by those neighboring eleven campuses. Monday morning breakfasts were sessions where more than one damsel would flaunt a new diamond engagement ring to the accompaniment of screeches from admiring, if not jealous, girlfriends.

Olga tried to transfer out of Shelton during her freshman year, so convinced was she that a significant educational mismatch had occurred. The guidance counselor warned her that she would be pegged by all prospective campuses as an indecisive quitter if she didn't at least give the place the mandatory minimum two years' endurance test. So, Olga hunkered down even harder with her studies, prepared to write off the first two years of her college career.

The Vietnam War was in its infancy. It was a time when opposing sides wrote and spoke civilly to each other, on the merits, even though vehemence was building. Olga had chosen her own position—against the war—after reading a history of how long the French had been mired in the very same location under a different name, the Indochina War.

At Shelton, those who studied government were considered "grunges"—the equivalent of today's brainiacs or nerds. There wasn't enough technology around yet to consider them full-blown geeks. A group of her peers had decided to organize a school-wide debate on the pros and cons of the war. One member of the group, a far more rabid anti-war activist, was prepared to do verbal battle, but the faculty required that the debate include someone on the pro-war side of the issue. They invited one young girl who had been active in the Young Republicans primarily because of her family's influence in the GOP (Grand Old Party—Republican) over the years. The group legitimized the session by inviting a faculty member to moderate between the two debaters.

The night of the debate came, and each side expected a slam-dunk verbal victory over the other side. What amazed Olga was that this bastion of social debs and dating managed somehow to put their preening and mating priorities on a back burner for one night to attend a serious debate on a subject that ultimately would influence their lives for decades to come. The hall was full to capacity. The debate was civil and serious. The issue was discussed with the respect it warranted. And all listened and learned what political deliberation could be.

There was no clear winner that night, just as there was no clear path out of the quagmire of Vietnam for another fifteen years. Olga remembered feeling not bad about "her side" not having taken the room by storm because she was so impressed by the sincerity and equanimity of the young woman who spoke on the side of the debate with which Olga could not quite agree—but which she could respect. Olga learned a great deal from her and has always held her in high regard as a genuine, thinking, and intelligent leader.

It is not necessary to agree with everything that a leader has to say. However, it is important to respect her. Almost 40 years later, that same woman described that evening in her own words this way:

> . . . *most college campuses were isolated from the unrest [surrounding the Vietnam War]. . . During my sophomore year, in the spring of 1966, I was one of two student members on a campus-wide student—faculty panel discussion politely termed, "Vietnam: Where Do We Go from Here?" I supported the war effort; I felt what we were doing—trying to prevent the expansion of communism throughout Southeast Asia—was in our national interest. In retrospect, I still believe we were in Vietnam for a worthy, even noble, cause, even if our strategy for engagement was flawed, as it so clearly was. The major lesson that Vietnam holds for America is that we must never go to war without a plan to win, not just the war but also the peace, a lesson reinforced by the challenges in Iraq after the fall of Baghdad.*[2]

Christie Todd Whitman also is a corporate board member at S.C. Johnson & Sons, Inc., Texas Instruments, United Technologies, and the Millennium Challenge Corporation. She is the former director of the U.S. Environmental Protection Agency, January 2001 to May 2003, and former governor of New Jersey from 1994 to 2001.

Lesson: Even in the days when it was expected that "the nice men would take care of us," we listened to our own good sixth sense about our own goals and objectives. We can genuinely disagree, but we learn the most when we discuss, debate, and listen to each other sincerely.

HOW CHANGE HAPPENS

Tracy wanted to attend graduate school and was searching for the right career track. Would it be business or science or technology? Wherever she looked, she kept hearing about the lack of women in the tenure track at graduate schools. Tracy began to wonder if she would be welcome in these non-typical career paths for women. Would she confront traditional barriers, or were there graduate schools that were finally making substantive change happen? In March 1999, the Massachusetts Institute of Technology (MIT) reported on a four-year intense effort by senior female faculty, Women in the School of Science, and senior leadership to address *and* to begin to resolve the "inequities that female faculty faced"[3] for decades at MIT.

Lotte Bailyn, professor at MIT, described the history, the process, and the results in her paper, "Academic Careers and Gender Equity: Lessons Learned from MIT."[4] Professor Bailyn's work is unique in that it does not simply make demands; it does not represent a negative "marching with placards" demonstration in opposition. It does represent an effective and reasoned approach to solving complex problems arising out of the fact that people from different backgrounds and perspectives have different expectations.

Professor Bailyn's paper presents three perspectives:

1. Clarifying the definition of gender inequity as a problem that can be addressed by civilized people of both genders.
2. Describing how MIT accomplished something worthwhile.
3. A roadmap that other academic *or* corporate organizations of conscience *could* pursue if they truly wished to address their similar problems of gender inequity at their establishments.

She described what she termed an "integrated vision of gender equity"

   . . .based on integration rather than separation of the public spheres of economic work and the private sphere of family, community, and other personal involvements.[5]

She described two possible ways of looking at "gender equity" in institutions like academia:

- "[One definition] . . . equates equity with equality: equal pay, equal access to opportunities to enter an occupation and to advance in it, and freedom from harassment."
- The second definition "is based on fairness": "In other words, merely allowing women faculty to meet the criteria for academic success, on terms that have been defined by men and represent their life experiences does not guarantee equity."[6]

MIT research found that most senior women faculty at MIT were not married and did not have children, unlike the situation at many bio-tech firms, which actually did a better job, in some instances, at integrating work-family balance into their employees' lives.

Professor Bailyn acknowledged that despite great goals and efforts at MIT and at other academic establishments, inequities persisted, but *not* for the reasons most would cite:

- not because women do not have the skills, interests, etc. to accomplish scientific work.
- *and not* because men intentionally discriminate because they do not want to share power.

She suggested that "more subtle dynamics . . . are at work . . . both on the individual and the institutional level."[7]

Professor Bailyn provided a comprehensive overview of the efforts at MIT from 1994 through 2003. At one point, MIT's president invited presidents from eight other research universities, their provosts, and two women faculty from each campus to spend one day discussing "women in academic science and engineering."

After much dialog, three goals were agreed upon and defined:

1. to have the number of women on their faculty mirror the number of women they educate; to stop the "leaking pipeline"—the erosion of women in technical fields as they progressed up the faculty career ladder;
2. to ensure that those women already on their faculty have an equally positive experience as their men; to stop the "marginalization"—the exclusion of women from mainstream career activity; and

3. to have no faculty member—male or female—disadvantaged by family
    responsibilities, whether it be for children, elders, or partners.[8]

Not only did MIT bring the issues to the table, but they also broadened the experiential base by including other relevant campuses, and they used those resources to fully and fairly redefine the challenge that they all faced.

The universities that were included were the cream of the crop: Cal Tech, Stanford, University of California at Berkeley, University of Michigan, Penn, Princeton, Yale, and—yes, even Harvard. That Harvard was part of this process and yet Dr. Lawrence Summers felt he had the right to pontificate unilaterally on the subject as he did in January 2005 provides new perspective on why some of the female faculty opted to walk out in disgust.

What MIT learned, and Dr. Summers demonstrated with force, was described by Virginia Valian in her book, *Why So Slow? The Advancement of Women.*[9] Professor Bailyn quoted Valian on the existence of "gender schemas" in the minds of men and women in private and institutional/organizational settings:

> *[gender schemas are] the implicit, largely non-conscious beliefs about sex differences that all of us, men and women alike, share.*[10]

For example, as a result of "gender schemas," "men are consistently overrated, while women are underrated."[11] These beliefs persist even in the face of readily available information to the contrary.

Later on, Malcolm Gladwell, in his book *Blink: The Power of Thinking without Thinking,*[12] described an orchestra of a major metropolitan area that realized that it had too few women. In an effort to increase their share of women musicians, the orchestra held auditions where the candidates were asked to play from behind a screen—to hide their gender. The orchestra was surprised when it learned that it still had failed to dramatically change the gender ratios until it realized that the judges continued to differentiate among the candidates by the sound of the high heels of women musicians as they walked across the stage floor. Only after the orchestra installed silencing carpeting in the auditioning rooms was it possible to have truly "blind" and objective auditions. The number of women musicians increased dramatically once talent became the sole criteria for acceptance into the orchestra.

MIT did the only thing it could to get out of the "gender inequity bind"— it looked at the problem with all of its ugly warts and constructed a roadmap out of gender inequity. Professor Bailyn reported that,

All of [the] assumptions and the practices [about competence and success in academic institutions] were built upon the practices and norms constructed around the life experiences of men. . . . All of these assumptions and the practices associated with them disadvantaged academic women. But they are so ingrained and so taken for granted that one forgets that they are not God-given, but are constructed by mere men . . . and may have some unintentional consequences for the university mission.[13]

Once the institution recognized that the risks were larger than merely salary schemes but might actually limit the ability of the institution to perform to its full potential, then the institution started to accept the possibility that it might be cutting off more than a digit and may actually be cutting into an essential artery.

MIT applied what Professor Bailyn called "an integrated gender lens" to remedy the unjustified inequities it found there. It was not a fast process, nor is the job complete; but the roadmap they used is worthy and ready for use by any institution of conscience which truly wishes to find its way out, as well.[14]

1. **A committed champion:** The champion was one woman scientist who finally had had enough, who wouldn't take this stuff anymore, and who was willing and committed to do something to fix the situation.

2. **A point of connection:** That first woman found one other like-minded woman scientist willing to join her and to broaden the dialog among other women faculty in science.

3. **Collecting data:** The women opted to involve the dean (a male) to appoint a committee to collect the data systematically and comprehensively, rather than "go it alone" and risk missing a lot of data under the dean's control.

4. **Working with the dean:** The dean not only had the data but he also had the power to fix things—to achieve their goals of redress and remedy.

5. **Appointing the committee:** Senior women from each department were included on the committee *and* some men—a condition to which the women agreed *only* if the men were powerful enough to implement solutions.

6. **The findings:** The results of the research provided "a convincing picture" that—initially—was evaluated and shared privately within the university.

7. **From private to public:** Two years after the initial report was prepared (and five years after the initial committee was formed), a narrative report was released to the public at large.

8. **The media:** The university finally took the discussion into the greater community, the public domain, and involved the media, which showed itself to be both respectful of the process and worthy of its presentation.

MIT is not yet what would be considered "gender equity heaven." But it has the respect of the Women in the School of Science because it took the initiative rather than simply accept the status quo. MIT thereby has provided universities, globally, with a real process and a roadmap to address the challenge they all face.

Lesson: It is much harder to build solutions to the problems that originate from our past failures to build effective collaborations. Leaders and mentors are those who roll up their sleeves and make change happen.*

WOMEN IN LEADERSHIP BUSINESS CASE STUDIES

We are educating our young women to search for comfort and some elusive sense of "balance." We are educating our young men for competition. In classrooms, we invite young women "to express their opinions . . . Explore lingering questions." In those same classrooms, we prepare our young men to research facts, construct and deconstruct cases, challenge, and be challenged intellectually; to stand up and to speak out. We teach our young men to debate. We teach our young women to play nice.

We teach our young women to foster a thought-provoking dialog that makes everyone feel at ease. We foster and enhance our young men's performance and ability to produce solutions in a challenging world. We encourage our young women to volunteer and to serve. We teach our young men to strive and to succeed.

So why should we be surprised when our young women enter the business environment and essentially have to start back at square one to teach themselves, alone, how to analyze, understand and deal with real-world complexities and challenges in a globally competitive marketplace?

A solution is to teach women to analyze business challenges using business cases based on contemporary women in leadership. Not merely Oprah, Martha, or Suzi. Not Andrea or Miranda. Real women in real business.

---

*Excerpts reprinted with permission from *Academic Careers and Gender Equity: Lessons Learned from MIT* by Lotte Bailyn. Copyright © 2003, John Wiley and Sons.

Who founded Gymboree? Koala Corporation? F-International? Did they succeed? How and why? How do these women corporate leaders compare to the founder of Build-A-Bear Workshop? Are these real economic businesses, or are they play-at-home made big? Is there a Montessori business case that describes the concept of train-the-trainer as a business education model? Why *not* a business case on Hewlett-Packard from a "women in leadership" perspective: Carly Fiorina *and* Pat Dunn? What did we learn about governance from their experiences?

There are just a few business cases about successful women in leadership. Most Harvard Business case studies "use" women in stereotypical roles in typical, middle-management and supporting positions. They discuss the "powder puff" problems of human resources: choosing whom to fire and how, soft skills of customer support or service, and women who "passionately" pursue feeding or saving the world.

A few notable exceptions include the Donna Dubinski business case from Darden School of Business, University of Virginia: the story of a high-technology business woman who was instrumental in the founding of the PalmPilot Co. Another example is the story of Deborah Coleman's rise to chief financial officer at Apple Computer, Inc.

There are a host of other incredible women in leadership candidates about whom we could develop real business case material:

Dawn Lepore, CEO of drugstore.com, former CIO of Charles Schwab

Darla Moore, financial wizard who established a school of business in South Carolina

Kay Koplovitch, a prominent businesswoman who founded the USA Network and Springboard Enterprises

Esther Dyson, Wall Street technology analyst, angel investor, founder of EDVenture Holdings, which publishes *Release n.0*—her blog and technology books and newsletters

Pat Summitt, now head coach emeritus of the Tennessee Lady Vols [Volunteers], the winningest woman's basketball team in history

Charlene Barchefsky, senior international partner at the law firm Wilmer Cutler Pickering Hale and Dorr LLP and U.S. trade representative named by President Bill Clinton.

Dina Dublon, former CFO at JP Morgan Chase and director at major US technology firms

Diana Lady Dougan, the first statutory U.S. coordinator for international communications and information policy

Adelia A. Coffman, one of the original founders of Qualcomm Inc., a major semiconductor company

Pat Mitchell, current president and chief executive officer of the Paley Center for Media and formerly the president and CEO of Public Broadcasting Service (PBS)

And if some of these names do not ring the familiar bell of recognition, that speaks volumes about how our educational, information, and media institutions have failed to portray successful women.

Female role models abound, but women need to develop the business case mentality that uses concrete facts and information as the foundation for debate and deliberation on leadership issues. Business case materials can be more dynamic today than ever before using contemporary delivery tools and technologies to capture the attention and interest of today's media-savvy business school student.

The challenge is not simply to entertain, but rather to use the technology effectively and holistically to capture and deliver all the complex nuances, issues, and perspectives that surround problem-solving in our contemporary society.

"Education is the preservation of that which the race deems indispensable," is the message carved into the concrete above the Royce Hall stage at UCLA—the words of the first chancellor. Our failure as an educational institutions to allow intellectual examination of the work, accomplishments, and achievements of women in business at many public and private schools of business is a major shortcoming.

Lesson: The greatest numbers of mentors are the women who are succeeding in business every day today. We can capture their wisdom and pass that on to the next generation of young men *AND WOMEN* through the powerful vehicle of business case studies.

THREE

At Play: Mentorship in Sports

Games and entertainment provide some of the most memorable opportunities for learning and for mentoring. Not only is play the most relaxing medium in which to learn, but play provides conditioning and error-corrective mechanisms almost secretly. Coaches are the mentors in play. They may be fathers or brothers. And a few are women.

Young girls finally have the opportunity to play at group games where they learn sportsmanship, competition, and the joy of teamwork. They also are learning that it is their own performance that will "get them into the game." The mentorship of young girls in sports in schools has only been apparent since 1972, just over forty years ago, when the passage of Title IX meant that financial revenue received through taxation of everyone would be returned equally to that same base in the form of federally funded subsidies of sports in education.

Enabling legislation just enables. The reason young girls now are mentored in sport is because of the contributions of women such as Patsy T. Mink and Billie Jean King and the athletic achievements of women like Joanie Benoit Samuelson and Kathrine Switzer.

The games we give to our children either teach them to think in stereotypical boxes or expand their horizons and guide them to explore and experiment with life, technology, and their potential.

Sporting events and celebrations of champions present opportunities to aspire to higher levels of achievement. Great mentors are the ones who encourage us to rise to those levels rather than be intimidated by the comparison with ourselves or our performance at this time.

We have come a long way, thanks to the mentorship of both family and strangers. Our daughters will take the lessons of play, teamwork, and competition much further than we could possibly imagine.

THE GAME OF KICKBALL

Jane reports that women often tell her they feel "left out":

* they don't feel accepted in the business world;
* they don't feel part of the informal networks;
* therefore, gender-based discrimination must exist.

She suggests playing devil's advocate—to do something really different by trying to image what it must be like to be a little girl who sees that there are a lot of little boys playing kickball out there on the school playground.

"Wow! That looks like fun! I could do that, I bet!" the little girl says to herself.

First, she goes to all the other little girls on the playground and asks them, "Why don't we play kickball?"

They answer, "Ugh! That's a boy's game. They *never* let any of us girls play with them. Why do you want to do that? Come play with us and have fun!"

But Jane is curious about kickball because it seems to be a lot more fun than any other games that she's seen on the playground. So she goes over and stands on the sidelines of the kickball game, hoping to be asked to join in the game. The boys continue playing together, ignoring her.

That night, she goes home and complains to her big sister, saying, "I want to play kickball with the boys, but they won't invite me to play with them!"

Drawing from her wealth of playground experience, her big sister says, "Tell the teacher she has to make the boys let you play."

Next day, Jane goes to the teacher, who agrees that the boys *should* let her play. The teacher tells the little boys to let her play kickball with them. They do so, until the teacher walks away. Then the boys all walk away as if the game were over. The little girl realizes she's being gamed. The boys don't like to be forced to include her.

The next night, she goes back to her mother, who, wise woman that she is, tells her, "If you want to play with the boys, first, you need to learn how they play the game. What are the rules of their game?"

So the little girl goes back and watches the game from the sidelines, trying to figure out how the rules work. She talks with a few of the boys, asking good questions, and they answer her. When the ball comes her way, she kicks it back really hard to the pitcher. The boys discover that she is a pretty good kicker. A couple of days later, another ball comes her way, and she tosses the ball back. They see that she can throw the ball, too.

So, one day, the captain of a team takes a chance and asks her to be on their side. She gets a couple of good kicks in during the day but then gets tagged out really hard as she's running the bases. That night she goes home, complaining to her mother about how tough it is playing kickball.

Her mother, wise woman that she is, tells her, "If you want to play with the boys, you're going to have to expect to get bumped around sometimes."

So, the girl goes back, gets on the team, gets some bumps, bruises, and other red badges of courage. She realizes that kickball *is* fun. She realizes that she *can* learn the rules of the game. She realizes that she *can* play the game. She realizes that, by staying in the game, she *can* perform with the best of them and that she *improves* as a player.

Lesson: What are we telling our daughters, our young leaders, and our women in top management? Are we telling them they *can* succeed *if* they are willing to learn the rules of corporate life, *if* they are willing to endure some of the expected challenges of that experience?

THE SOFTBALL THROW

The Fourth of July was a fairground event that drew families from every nook and cranny of Elena's little town, southwest of Boston. The year after she turned twelve, the Independence Day festivities included foot races, relay races, potato sack races, three-legged races, and for the first time ever, a softball throw for girls aged twelve to thirteen years.

Elena was a major tomboy, having been trained and coached by her older two brothers, her father, and even occasionally by her mother (a former catcher from the family league). Elena played *real* baseball with her older brothers for several years and knew the sharp sting of the smaller sphere in the pocket of her well-worn, hand-me-down glove. She had been taught to throw the ball *right*, darn it. Not like a girl, for Pete's sake.

And now it was the big day when Elena could throw the ball for the blue ribbon. Each girl had two tries. About ten girls had lined up for their first throw.

Elena's father was coaching her in the last few minutes before her turn. "Don't worry," he said. "It's just a little bigger than you're used to."

Then, with his massive hand rolling around the tiny orb, her father filled Elena's head with what seemed to be a hundred separate instructions about how to place her fingers on the ribbed stitching, how to plant her feet, how to put her whole body into a geometrically perfect projectile motion. When it was Elena's turn to toss the ball, her head swam trying to recall all of his instructions.

With the huge softball dwarfing her hand, Elena stepped up to her place and threw the shortest, flattest, pancake flop of a toss—the worst performance ever. Worse than the frilliest of girls who had preceded her.

Disaster was written all over her father's face. He turned and walked away. Elena crept back to the end of the line, head hanging, wishing the day were over so that she could crawl under a mound of earth and just rot away.

The next girl threw "just like a girl" but farther than Elena had done.

"Why did I do so poorly?" Elena asked herself. Her mind went back to summers in the lower field. She saw her brothers hitting long, lo-o-o-ng balls to her, standing in the middle of their center field. She would catch the ball, and then—with all her might—throw it back with *just one bounce* before it reached the batter. Elena remembered playing "pepper" with them. One brother would hit a short, fast, one-bounce ground ball to her; she'd grab it and throw with all her strength to the other brother, who would pitch it to the hitter, and the cycle would start all over again. And again and again and again, until it was so dark they couldn't see each other anymore. Elena *knew* how to throw the ball, darn it!

She was jolted out of her memories by the event judge, who was calling to her to take her second turn. "Are you ready?"

She caught the ball he tossed to her and moved into position for her last attempt. Barely perceptible in the distance, Elena heard something that sounded like her name.

"Out here, toss it to me," said a voice from the distance. And there he was: at about the distance from home to second base, her father was standing and waving his arms, challenging her to throw the ball that far.

Elena threw the ball with all the natural might she could muster from afternoons and evenings of joyous play. She watched her father look up and over his shoulder as the ball passed him, sailing overhead in a high, floating arch. He looked back and cheered.

Lesson: Tell me "how to" do it when I have the luxury to listen and to learn, to make mistakes, and to correct myself in play. Then, when it is time to perform, give me a mighty goal to which I may aspire and, hopefully, exceed.

GOOD FOR THE HEART

Taking a brisk afternoon walk is supposed to be good for one's heart, doctors say. At a nearby playground, ten- to twelve-year-old girls were playing baseball under the guiding tutelage of some dad-coaches. Baseball—the game with the small, hard ball. Every girl on the field had a helmet. Some had kneepads. It was not a game—it was practice.

The girls were working very hard, developing specific skills. One dad-coach was working with a small line of girls facing him. The first girl was practicing swinging her bat. He was holding a long pole with a baseball attached to the end, painted bright iridescent yellow, extending out a one-foot length beyond the pole. Each girl would get into the proper at-bat stance then swing her bat at the bright yellow ball—about a dozen times. They were learning hand-eye coordination: putting the bat where the ball was located. Focus, positioning, balance, persistence. Hit the ball. Again. Again. Again. "Great job," dad-coach would encourage her and then help the next girl with her stance and swing.

Another dad-coach was with a different line-up of little girls over by third base. He would toss an arched pitch in slow motion while another dad-coach played catcher. Each girl would swing at the moving missile, judging timing, distance, and speed. Again. Again. Again.

A third dad-coach was on the mound pitching real baseballs to little-girl batters who now had to apply what they had just learned from the smaller circles to the real world: faster pitches, real swings, real hits, real misses.

Crack! The ball went sailing into the field, where another little girl caught it. Another pitch. A swing and a miss. Another pitch. *Crack*! Again. Again. Again.

Lesson: This is how young women learn about challenge, risk, and competition. They stand at the plate and tune their stance. They learn to keep their eye on the ball—on the goal. They learn to endure repetition until they "feel" it is right. They learn that a hit and a miss are the same thing. These are the young women who will lead us tomorrow, who will face tomorrow's tests in the real world, away from the playground.

ON TITLE IX

"Those who cannot remember the past are condemned to repeat it."[1]

What about those who never even bothered to learn about the past in the first place?

A newspaper article[2] reviewed Karen Blumenthal's book, *Let Me Play: The Story of Title IX: The Law That Changed the Future of Girls in America*.[3] The book presented the history of the federal legislation that in 1972 gave women in college and public schools the opportunity to access taxpayer dollars on an equal footing with male athletes. At the end of the article, Jennifer Capriati, the talented U.S. tennis star, was quoted responding to the question of whether she had any inspiring words for President Bush as he considered potential restrictions on Title IX. Her reply: "I have no idea what Title IX is."

Today, in walking by neighborhood playgrounds on any afternoon, one can see hundreds of little girls of all ages playing on the softball and soccer fields. They are fully garbed in uniforms, shin-guards and head-gear. They're in the batter's box, perfectly poised and eyes ahead, ready to knock the oncoming pitch square ahead and over the fence. Today's young female pitchers use the "windmill pitch"—an underarm fast whirlybird windup—rather than the over-the-shoulder pitch that was more natural for their brothers.

It is a marvel how far we have come from the days before the passage of the Educational Amendments of 1972 with Title IX, which banned sex discrimination in programs and activities at any school that receives federal taxpayer money.

In that past, typically there were just one or two girls who even wanted to participate in team sports. They played in their own jeans and Keds. Most were taught by brothers who would yell, "Don't throw like a *girrrrlllll*!" They taught sisters how to throw the ball with a full wind-up over the shoulder. They taught them not to shy away from the pitch coming full bore across the plate. They taught them how to keep their eye on the ball, watching it all the way to the bat. They taught them how to time that step into the pitch. They taught them to let the weight of the bat carry itself in one smooth stroke toward and through the ball to the very farthest fence.

Much later, high school gym teachers taught the "windmill pitch" to girls' softball players. Brothers, too, learned how much more powerful and accurate the "windmill pitch" could be and adopted it in the slow-pitch softball leagues of young adults. But that was much later. Much later.

Today, on softball and soccer fields in every town and village, it is a wonderful sight to see hundreds of young girls learning how to play on a team. They are learning how to cheer for their peers—how to share the glory. They are learning the rigor and discipline of a position, the precision of batting, the power of pitching, the intricacy of plays, the concepts of strategy, and the beauty of teamwork. They are learning how to have fun and get a little messy in the process. They are learning to deal with victory and defeat—to "meet Triumph and Disaster and treat those two imposters the same."[4].

And there they are, again—brothers and fathers. They're out there on the field, at the girls' side, telling them how to "do it right." They are once again our daughters' mentors, out on today's softball and soccer fields. They are teaching them the "rules of the game." They are teaching them how to love sport and everything in it.

Lesson: There are many sisters and mothers who are not out there on the playing field helping our brothers and fathers to do this most important mentoring job. To them we must ask, "Have you forgotten the past, or did you just miss that lesson altogether?"

BILLIE JEAN KING

Most people acknowledge Billie Jean King as an outstanding tennis athlete with 129 career titles, of which six were at singles events at Wimbledon and four were U.S. Open singles titles. Others remember her from the 1973 Battle of the Sexes tennis match where she beat Bobby Riggs at his own game of hype, simply wearing the guy down in three straight sets.

Even more important than these personal victories is the fact that every woman tennis player on the circuit today owes King a debt of gratitude for making it possible for women to earn as much as men in major U.S. tennis events. King, with Rosie Casals and seven other world class women tennis players, established the Women's Tennis Association in June 1973, just a week before Wimbledon. Meeting in Gloucester, England, they used their leadership as leverage to negotiate prize money for women on a par with that paid to male competitors.[5]

In her book, *Pressure is a Privilege*,[6] King describes the challenges faced and overcome—including the intransigence of other women champions of that day. If women want to break the back of income differentials for the same or comparable performance, they will pool their talent and leverage that power in direct negotiations for their due. And by doing so, successfully, everyone with an interest in the outcome will benefit: competitors, advertisers, fans, the next generation of players, and the sport itself.

Lesson: In order to "beat the system," you have to be willing to work together to put a new system into place in its stead.

JOAN BENOIT SAMUELSON

One warm summer day, August 5, 1984, Joanie Benoit flashed by as Patricia watched the first official Olympic Women's Marathon held in Los Angeles. Pat was on a bicycle, and Joanie, surprisingly short and lean, was in a white painter's cap. She was running ever so easily, several seconds ahead of the other 49 women headed southbound on Ocean Avenue toward Marina del Rey, back to the Coliseum and into the history books.

There was sweet justice to Benoit's achievement. Those who were watching her remembered another day, almost 20 years earlier (1967), when Boston Marathon officials, realizing they had issued a bib number to a female runner, tried unsuccessfully to physically remove Kathrine Switzer from the race.[7] It was Switzer who had presented the case to the Executive Committee of the International Olympic Committee, ensuring that the women's marathon would be included in the 1984 Summer Olympic Games held in Los Angeles. It took almost two decades, but Switzer and her peers made change happen.

It's hard to believe, today, that rules once forbade men and women from competing in the same race. There were rules barring women from races of more than one and a half miles. Benoit and Switzer are role models, not just as marathon record holders, but, rather, because they said, "What do you *mean* 'women can't'?"

That is the belief that was handed down to Pat from the Olympic role models of 1958, when Mildred (Babe) Didrikson startled the track world with her record-setting shorter distance events. Pat's family called her "Babe," too, because she ran everywhere when she was a gangly young girl.

Five years after the Los Angeles Olympics of 1984, Pat's husband tossed a newspaper clipping in front of her at the breakfast table. It said, "Go from the Couch to the Coliseum. Train to Run the City of L.A. Marathon with the L.A. Leggers®."[8]

Joanie and Babe flashed by her again.

The ad was for The L.A. Leggers®' marathon training program, which was created by Bob Scott, radio announcer of KNX1070 Newsradio, together with Olympic distance runner Jeff Galloway. They teamed up to create a 30-week conditioning program to teach average Joes and Janes how to complete a full marathon without injury. Scott was radio commentator for the first four City of L.A. Marathons and saw that too many amateur runners failed to properly train for the 26.2-mile (40-kilometer) distance. They'd drop like flies at the first hill. If they made it past that point, most untrained runners would drop out at the proverbial eighteenth mile "brick wall."

Pat and her husband had been trying to lose excess weight packed on at too many corporate cafeteria lunches. Over that breakfast together, they agreed that they'd just start jogging with the group, run up to maybe 10 miles, and then let the other runners continue to train for the full marathon without them. They signed up, became volunteers, trained for the full 30 weeks, and finished their first marathon together—beaming at each other from under their own white painters' caps as they crossed the finish line at the Coliseum, just like Joanie Benoit had done.

Two years later, Bob Scott was ready to retire from KNX1070, the LA Leggers®, and Los Angeles. Pat and her husband had continued as volunteers. All of the runners were invested in the program and did not want to see it fade away or be co-opted by other interests. So, they incorporated. They formed a board of directors from the average Joes and Janes. They met at night for weeks on end during the summer of 1991. The board was hopeful and afraid at the same time. Methodically, they pushed forward through one tedious agenda, committee, or budget item after another—just as each had trained to do for 30 weeks at a clip. Together they rebuilt the program into an institution that survives today. Thousands of men and women now achieve what was once considered unthinkable: they run and finish a marathon without injury. They don't just quit at the first hill—that first challenging obstacle. They cross the finish line, beaming, just like Joanie Benoit did on that amazing August morning.

In training for the City of L.A. Marathon, members of the LA Leggers® learned to eliminate the word "only" from their vocabulary. To say that you ran "only" one or ten miles trivialized the accomplishment, disparaged the effort, and undermined the mental attitude needed to continue on this significant path.

Lesson: There will always be "only" a few at the beginning of a major wave of change. It didn't matter that Babe Didrikson was "only" the first woman to compete in major track and field events or that Joanie Benoit was "only" one among a handful of women running in that first Women's Marathon of the Olympics. What matters is how we finish.

THE GAME OF LIFE

Hasbro, the East Longmeadow, Massachusetts, game-maker, re-designed some of its old board games to meet contemporary needs. It's fun to remember the old games. It's even more interesting to see how the new games reflect a truly changed perspective on historic problems. According to *The Wall Street Journal* "In the Lead" columnist, Carol Hymowitz:

> *Another classic, The Game of Life, was revised to reflect consumers' wishes for more balanced lives. In the original game, success equaled money and the winner was the player who earned the most. In the new game, players move among four quadrants: to "live it" and have adventures, to "love it" and have family lives, to "learn it" and become educated, and also to "earn it."*[9]

At least in the game world, today, we see that there are multiple paths to personal and professional success. We're giving individuals the opportunity to define their unique track. In the twenty-first century, the possible tracks are now four: adventure, family, education, and achievement. "Diversity" is now used to describe the fact that different people might wish to pursue different goals at different levels of achievement.

There once was a time when some innovative women, such as Felice Schwartz, advocated something very much along these same lines. Some of the more zealous among us chose to excoriate her and to shut her up, much to our great loss. Just think about what might have been possible if we'd accepted the ideas that she put forth over twenty years ago about the idea that there might be two possible tracks to success—for women of achievement.

Felice Schwartz (the founder in 1962 of Catalyst Inc., the New York-based nonprofit advocate for women's advancement to leadership), in the January 1989 issue of the *Harvard Business Review*, recommended that employers separate female candidates into two categories. Women who were interested in what she called the "career-primary" track would be groomed for top-level positions. The women who were interested in the "career and family" path would be encouraged to pursue midlevel positions with shorter hours and possibly part-time jobs.[10]

Feminist critics hammered Schwartz's proposal, calling the alternative path "the Mommy Track," saying that that alternative would relegate women workers to a second-class status (the so-called "pink ghetto") and would possibly violate antidiscrimination laws.[11]

Schwartz realized then that not all women wanted to pursue corporate career paths. We are still stuck with the consequences of not giving her thoughts the attention they warranted. Instead, today, we persist in trying to provide a "one size fits all" set of solutions for women's aspirations, rather than work with the talent we're given and enable each individual to achieve the level that is right and appropriate for her aspirations.

We're wasting money and effort trying to provide "women incentive networks" for all women in corporate hierarchies, many of whom have no internal motivation to aspire to corporate leadership roles. We're trying to fit all round women into our very limited subset of square peg holes, and it's simply not working.

Not all women want to be corporate board directors. Nor do all women want to focus on family and children. Why can't both of those options be viable choices for the next generation of females aspiring to be the best they can be? Why do the sisters who want "work-family balance" have anything to say about how the "corporate governance" sisters prepare themselves for leadership? And vice versa? They are two separate tracks, paths, and options. They may overlap in one woman's life. They may be sequential in the life of another. They certainly can talk civilly with each other.

Nor is it necessary that one subsidize the other's aspirations. Choose one path and pursue it to the best of your capabilities. Choose the other and do likewise. Try to do both at the same time, and it probably will be more difficult, but still feasible. Just don't expect that we tax one path to ensure that the other path is "easy" or feasible for "all."

Lesson: The Game of Life means each person gets to choose from among the multiple paths to personal and professional success. Not everyone will agree. Everyone needn't pay for everyone else's choices.

THE LEMONADE STAND

In the late 1970s, the Apple II Plus microcomputer dominated the marketplace for personal computing. The PC wasn't even a glint in the eyes of IBM at the time. For about a decade, Apple provided a copy of an introductory economics game called *The Lemonade Stand* with each computer sold.

The Lemonade Stand was written in the BASIC language and was one of the very first software games.[12] The program staked you with $3.00 on the first "day." You were told how much it cost to make each glass of lemonade (sometimes your mother would help by giving you the sugar). You were told the weather forecast: sunny, cloudy, rainy, whatever. You could buy advertising signs for 25 cents each to attract attention to your stand. And you decided how many glasses to make and how much to charge customers for each glass. Once you made all your decisions, you'd "run" the program and learn how well business went for that "day." Maybe the weather forecast was wrong. Maybe the customers weren't thirsty, so you didn't sell all of the glasses you made. Maybe you put out too few or too many signs, or maybe the wind blew them away. The program calculated your "daily profit" based on all your combined decisions (price) times (glasses sold) minus (costs per glasses made) minus (costs per advertising sign) times (number of signs made) and the risks you faced. You kept playing the program for 30 days or until you wiped out.

This was a fascinating introduction to micro-economics. It was so simple, but so intriguing to see what the random nature of a new "day" would produce. Adults and kids alike delighted in playing the game. Some youngsters would display unique insight into the underlying economic factors *and* an enthusiasm for successfully growing profits every day.

Lemonade Stand provided the perfect vehicle to introduce the micro-computer to family and friends and to convince them that technology could be a fun and positive force in their life. One of the more talented youngsters to learn *The Lemonade Stand* went on to receive a doctorate in neuropsychiatry, doing functional MRIs of human brains to learn how they think, remember, and solve problems.

Lesson: This simple game provided today's personal computer entrepreneurs with the introduction to economics that they needed to become savvy business persons.

THE TAKE AWAY

On July 18, 2009, at the L.A. Coliseum, Ruth and her husband celebrated the twenty-fifth anniversary of the Los Angeles Olympics, the twenty-third international event that was held in 1984. In attendance for the anniversary event were 60 Olympians, representing games dating back to the 1950s, and including Mary Lou Retton, Nadia Comaneci, and Anita DeFrantz—the woman who was responsible for managing the LA84 Foundation over the past two and a half decades. The LA84 Foundation received $93 million at its inception 25 years ago and has invested $185 million in programs helping more than two million young people and seeded hundreds of youth athletic programs in schools and communities throughout Southern California. Joan Benoit Samuelson, the first woman gold medal winner in the first ever women's Olympic Marathon, was not able to attend but sent her congratulations. Four out of ten International Olympic Committee (IOC) board of director members are women (including Anita DeFrantz). Stephanie Streeter was named acting chief executive officer of the United States Olympic Committee on March 5, 2009. Ms. Streeter is an accomplished business executive who excelled during her competitive career in women's basketball.

With this as a backdrop to the evening, before the event, Ruth was snacking at a table on the Peristyle end of the Coliseum. At the same table was a young lady who introduced herself by saying, "You would be bored to hear me describe my job at a software company."

Ruth thought to herself, "How can she stand under the lights and the glory of these magnificent women of achievement and so denigrate herself to a total stranger? How have we taught young women today to 'take away' from themselves at the very moment they meet one who represents the cleanest possible slate of first impressions?"

Other companions for the evening (two men) exchanged their reasons for attending this marvelous occasion. Ruth listened and reminisced. When the conversation ebbed, she dared say to the young lady, "What persuaded you to think that I would not be interested in you, your job, or your company?" After pulling more from her about her firm, their products, and her position there, it happened that there were significant synergies between Ruth's interests and background and the young lady's current position.

Whoever taught this young lady to discount herself and her profession so thoroughly had harmed her grievously. Ruth thought, "I can only hope my pushiness and prodding—ever so slightly—might counterbalance that social conditioning. What if she had met another woman who understood how to play this game of 'debasement speak'? Would they both just stand there commiserating about the horror and tragedy of their gainful employment? How tragic."

Later, Ruth heard of a similar interview on National Public Radio with Sonia Sotomayor, where they proudly note that she—like the young girl at the event—was scared to death that people might discover she is an imposter. "I am always looking over my shoulder, wondering if I measure up."

Dr. Susan Murphy (in the book co-authored with Pat Heim, *In the Company of Women*) defined "The Imposter Syndrome" and described its psychological source.[13] Pauline Rose Clance and Suzanne Imes wrote about the concept in 1978.[14] Research indicates that the syndrome occurs equally among men and women. It reflects the disparity that exists when one's external power *exceeds* the person's self-esteem. To remedy the instasis, one can increase the self-esteem side of the equation or disperse the perception of power, which is exactly what happens when you imply you are "not measuring up."

Radio, television, and newspapers thrive on telling tales of how scary it is to come out from the kitchen, the back room, the bedroom. "Share with us and with Dr. Phil your deepest, darkest fears and trembling thoughts of failure and misery. Tell Oprah, dear heart, about how you know you are not up to this challenge, that everyone will soon discover that you are a fraud."

Michelle Obama and Sonia Sotomayor have both "confessed" to feeling insecure, scared to speak their minds, and afraid of being "found out."[15]

Lesson: Some role models offer parts we should decline. Even if media mavens, stars, and icons attempt to convey a negative message or "the take away," we should have the courage to challenge them.

GIMME *TEN*!

The young women athletes of Baylor and the University of Connecticut (UConn) were racing in a full court press. Tina Charles of the UConn Huskies drove ahead with the ball for a sweet lay-up. The crowd filled the stadium with a roar of appreciation.

The television camera panned to the seats just about midcourt where a mother and small girl (about eight years of age) stood smiling at each other in enthusiastic joy. You could read the mother's lips—"Gimme *ten*," she said, raising her hands barely to waist height, inviting her small companion to give her two "high fives." The young girl reached her hands up, slapping the two hands extended to her, then turned around and did the same thing to the adult man standing and cheering next to her. Mother, little girl, and maybe father all cheered the accomplishments of perhaps a sister or a student friend or possibly just the team they'd traveled to watch and encourage in San Antonio's NCAA Women's Basketball Semifinals.

How many ways have women progressed? How many huge, gigantic strides have they taken over the past three decades? Let us count the ways.

There was a time when girls who wanted to play sports were shunned and denigrated, viewed as aberrations and social misfits, even excluded from some educational institutions. Today, thanks to Representative Patsy Mink, who authored the Title IX Amendment of the Higher Education Act, over 30 percent of young women in high school now play team and competitive sports, where they learn how to perform under stress, keep their talents and wits about them, reach unprecedented goals, and learn invaluable real-world lessons. They also earn sports scholarships for college.

There once was a time when young girls who wanted to play basketball were forced to dribble *only* three times—any more would result in a forced turnover. Young women basketball players had to choose either to play defense *or* offence because each side was allowed to travel down to the midcourt line, then would screech to a halt and toss the ball to the other members of the team on the other side of the line. Playing full-court basketball, it was once believed, might physically undermine women's ability to bear children. Can anyone today imagine UConn's Maya Moore racing down to a theoretic midcourt limit and stopping?

There once was a time when young women athletes would play to empty bleachers, where neither fathers nor mothers cared how hard their young performers tried to excel. And as for television or media coverage—you've got to be kidding, right?

Today, both winter and summer Olympics now boast over 40 percent participation by women athletes. Today, television coverage and cheering crowd attendance are impressive. According to ESPN, television ratings for UConn's victory over Baylor on April 4, 2010, were up 37 percent from when the Huskies played in the semifinals a year earlier. The UConn-Baylor game drew a rating of 2.6, reportedly ESPN's best overnight rating for the Final Four in two years.

But, more than any of that, the difference between "way back then" and now is the ecstatic joy on the face of a small eight-year-old as she watches the outstanding performance of two excellent teams competing in the semifinals. She watches and learns about team work in a full-court, full-pressure framework. She watches young women being pushed, by their coaches and themselves, to execute and excel. She experiences the enthusiasm of thousands of fans surrounding her, celebrating that beautiful pivot, that short hook shot—that score.

And she turns, first to her mom, who joins her in this marvelous moment, saying "Gimme *ten!*" She turns around and shares the moment of victory with her dad or a friend. Look in her eyes and you will see joy, belief, and expectations.

Lesson: There is progress in our lives if we would but search to see it. A focus on past challenges should be undertaken only insofar as it permits us to see the distance we traveled to arrive at this height—and from which we may more clearly view the future.

FOUR

At Work: Mentors from Business to Careers

Where we work and with whom we work define a significant portion of our lives. We are surrounded by challenges, colleagues, and mentors. Knowing which is which constitutes the learning process. At work, we begin to apply the lessons provided to us by early mentors. We search for and find role models whom we might emulate.

There is a tendency to assume that all women are alike in their thoughts and expectations. Each woman has to determine and define what form of mentorship would be best for her, in her current position, whether she works at home or at an office.

Women who have found themselves at the most basic level of menial work may sometimes provide us with the best long-term financial advice. At a minimum, they teach us the dignity of work.

Foreign assignments, countries, and languages present themselves as learning opportunities. Mentors help guide us through the more treacherous terrain and enable us to build the confidence to undertake even greater challenges and uncertainty. Strangers can become teachers if we take the initiative to ask them to counsel us.

But mentors may not always respond as we might wish. They may be stuck in their own world, unable to escape their past habits and patterns.

The women we know may motivate us, inversely—teach us behaviors to avoid, teach us how *not* to present ourselves, professionally, if we wish to succeed. What, exactly, is the impression that would endure after an encounter?

Role models are the people we might seek to emulate because we see them as worthy. Our choice of people we admire defines who we are today and who we might become in the future. There are many women who have carved a clear path to financial self-sufficiency for other women, if we would only heed their wisdom.

There are great debates about how women make it to leadership roles. A certain amount of self-mentoring may be required. Women who have arrived can take on that task just as easily as men in the corporation. Being a change agent, whether that be within or outside of organizations and corporations, is an equally important path.

Women have contributed significantly to innovative fields of intellectual endeavor, including governance of cooperative space and telecommuting. Women entrepreneurs have begun to emerge in significant numbers thanks to the mentoring of both women and men business leaders.

QUANTITATIVELY DIFFERENT

A long time ago, one commentator suggested that every woman in an American household should go next door and contract with a neighbor's family to do exactly the same work that she previously performed in her own home. That small economic action would compel every family to value the work performed by female members of the economy who otherwise would do the work at home for free—uncompensated and underappreciated financially and emotionally.

Over the past 40 years, women's work has become more valued. Women who cooked meals at home for free now buy take-out and prepared meals and purchase "heat and eat" meals. As a result, meals away from home, today, constitute a multibillion-dollar business. Because food preparation is more highly valued, Iron Man Chefs have commercialized the simple task of cooking, added "sur la table" accoutrements, and mass-produced gizmos that take food preparation to near Xtreme Sports heights.

Women used to sew shirts, trousers, and dresses (and men made shoes). Today, the fashion industry is a mammoth economic sector with specialty wear spanning head to toes, from tots to the most senior among us.

Women used to pound their own organic herbs, spices, and powders together into fragrances, soaps, shampoos, coloring, and coverings. Now entire corporations specialize in one or more personal product sub-areas, all of which are billion-dollar revenue segments of the economy. And, after all, what is the size of the "incontinence" market?

Women used to be home-based teachers, then local school marms, and then public school teachers. Today, there are preschools, early childhood care centers, Montessori schools, charter schools, special needs education centers, and magnet schools focused on sciences, math, music, or another unique competency. There are extension educational programs at every major public university to train women and men in the business of managing child care facilities.

Women used to shave men's beards and trim the heads of all family members. Today, most men shave themselves, but the product selection of razors, soaps, lathers, and post-shaving products—for men and women alike—represents another multibillion-dollar consumables sub-sector. Today, almost everyone gets his or her hair cut by a specialist. There are barbers for men and salons that specialize in women or child hair care. Men are being attracted by the specialty hair care product market— whether metro males or otherwise. Manicures and pedicures, which used to be the preserve of the rich, are now a choice for the average middle class consumer, not to mention the seniors market. The decorative nail salon business, all by itself, is now the fastest growing economic opportunity for the female immigrant entrepreneur. There is a nail salon in almost every corner retail nook in the nation.

Next door to the nail salon is the dry cleaning establishment—another service formerly reserved for the wealthy, yet now an essential service for all economic classes. If there is no dry cleaner, then there is a coin-op laundry. Work formerly performed only by women has become work performed by everyone.

Women used to be the only caregivers: eldercare, nursing, and the whole range of healthcare support service professionals, as well as the office "assistant" or secretary. Technology has migrated most of the office assistant functions back to the individual worker or boss. If women are no longer in those professions today, it is because they found some higher bid for the value of their time with a commensurate reduction in the physical risks associated with the job. Today, nurses are being trained, educated, certified, and imported from overseas. Alternative-lifestyle real estate health facility options with support services are being created: senior residence centers, transitional medical facilities, and a wide variety of retirement housing options.

Alvin Toffler, in his book, *Future Shock*,[1] warned that the rate of change was increasing exponentially in our lives. One of the more dramatic pieces of evidence that "too much change too fast" can be overwhelming is when we realize that Toffler's book is now over 40 years old (written in 1970).

Women have been at the epicenter of a significant portion of the tectonic shifts taking place in work over these years. Women have been inundated with change in information, communication, education, careers, business, and home life.

The differences between what was then and what is now are huge if you stop to examine your grandmother's or mother's life compared to the life experienced by the typical female today. The same is true of fathers and sons, no doubt, but there has been much more continuity for men: a football game today is basically the same game that their fathers watched.

Women have been among the primary beneficiaries of that dramatic escalation of differences. As Toffler suggested, the greatest challenge facing economic actors would be the assimilation of the change: learning how to effectively incorporate differences arising over time into one's daily life.

Some women have struggled more than others with the rapid, sometimes frenetic, rate of change. Others have embraced it. Some have been taken for a whiplash ride while others have sailed on, well-balanced, on their own boards and under their own control.

Women who opt out in several possible stages of their lives are examples of those who struggle with the pace of change. Women who retire early; who leave corporate or work experience with no thought to continue producing, but rather just to rest; women who seek the slower pace of part-time work or who prefer the control of a home-schooling environment are simply those who are making one set of economic choices. Too often, we over-judge them and fail to acknowledge the legitimacy of their "different" decision making. They don't represent the whole economic spectrum of choices among women in the marketplace, but they do represent a quantifiable and analyzable subsector with measurable consequences to their choices. They are not Everywoman, as the mainstream media would wish us to believe. They are one type of buyer in the marketplace.

Other women embrace change—some more effectively than others. Paris Hilton, Britney Spears, and Lindsay Lohan ride change hell-bent for the effect. Many women thrive on the effect or appearance they create in the marketplace. Again, such women might represent a small quantifiable percentage of the whole, but the noise and splash created by their appearance is far larger than their actual numbers would indicate.

What share of the total marketplace is represented by women who have learned how to accommodate the rapid pace of change in our lives today? How many women successfully sail their own ship across these stormy seas? How many women somehow manage to traverse all the bumps and obstacles of contemporary life, and how do they keep their balance at such speeds?

In the past four decades, life has changed dramatically and has become exponentially better for women, especially. The value we place on the contribution women make to society has never been as high as it is today.

Do we segment "the female marketplace" with the same precision and understanding as we do others like, car buyers? Stocks vs. bond buyers? Too often we lump all women together in one huge, amorphous, meaningless agglomeration of sisterhood, rather than focus on the value created by specific subsectors.

Without a doubt, there also have been costs associated with these huge changes. But overall, our ability to solve contemporary problems and our willingness to do so have been enhanced by those women who choose to embrace the rapid pace of change rather than hide from it.

Today, we see a highly differentiated market of female economic actors, spanning a gigantic spectrum of behaviors and choices. Yet, we still try to tamp all women back into the easy-to-manage (and love) image of Mom, Apple Pie, Mother Teresa, and the Girl Back Home—or Hannah Montana or Paris Hilton or our Martha-Oprah-Suzie media imprint. When Katie Couric does not fit that media mold, we keep trying to pound her down until she fits back into the image that we believe will "sell" or "make us feel good."

There are huge quantitative differences among women today because, one by one, they stepped out of the house, out of the stereotypes, and out of the image-makers' molds. They also stepped out and beyond the reach of the feminist movement, which was simply a temporary way-station along the way to independent economic choices. We no longer need "a movement"—individual women today constitute the primary source of progress.

Lesson: There are significant and quantifiable economic differences that exist among women in today's marketplace. Perhaps it is time to stop trying to make all women appear to be the same. We might benefit by more efforts to survey, quantify, document, analyze, measure, and differentiate among women as independent economic actors, just as we would any other segment of the marketplace: housing, financial investment options, consumer choices, or food preferences.

ROSE MCNALLY

It was Laura's sophomore year in high school, and she needed a summer job. She was just old enough for a work permit, but not yet old enough to own a driver's license. All the classified ads in the newspaper wanted both of those and experience as well. She finally found a job posting for a chambermaid at a summer resort in East Falmouth, Massachusetts—"on the Cape." How hard could it be to make beds, sweep the floor, and wash the toilets? Laura wrote to the address and was offered the minimum wage job by return mail.

By the end of her "wise fool" year, Laura had become proficient at finding buses to her destinations and arrived at the East Falmouth Inn just in time to start her first real summer job. She was shown the workers' dormitory where she shared a room with three other waitresses. She unpacked her bag and went to bed early in order to be on deck to learn the ropes first thing next morning.

That's when Laura met her mentor—Rose McNally, the head chambermaid for the inn for the past hundred years or so. Rose walked with a crouch, a limp, and a lumber that bespoke her years laboring in the bedrooms and bathrooms of the wealthier guests of the Cape. Rose was dyed-in-the-wool Irish and spoke with a thick brogue as if she'd just gotten off the boat from County Cork. They met in the workers' dining room, consisting of a couple of tables just off the kitchen.

Rose sat by herself, off to the side. Her age and demeanor contrasted sharply with the young teenagers of the dining crew. Laura and Rose were the sole chambermaids at the inn.

Rose allowed Laura to finish her muffin and coffee and shuffled them both off to learn the fine art of tending to the living quarters of the inn's guests. Although pleasant in the early morning chit-chat at the dining table, Rose turned out to be a master sergeant on the job.

Laura learned how to make hospital corners on the beds by folding and refolding them time and time again until they met Rose's exacting standards. Rose expected taut sheets that could bounce a quarter. She didn't need a quarter, though, because she could tell a wrinkle a mile away. Laura had cleaned bathrooms at home and at school. She thought she was a pro until Rose inspected her work at the inn and found it wanting. Laura re-cleaned and re-re-cleaned toilets all morning until she satisfied Rose's expectations for perfection.

It continued like that for the first two weeks until Laura finally showed she could carry her own weight on the job. Rose didn't shirk from work with the addition of the second pair of hands. They were able to finish cleaning all of the units by early afternoon. They returned to the dining area for an afternoon "cuppa tea," and Rose became more loquacious than she had been while they worked.

Laura learned that Rose was now all alone. She's lost her husband years ago, and not long after that, one by one, her own three children had died too young. She wasn't complaining. She was just stating the facts of her life. She worked on the Cape in the summers, then relocated to inland resorts a little farther south during the winter months. She worked the year 'round. Laura couldn't guess her age, but she must have been in her late sixties. Social Security on a minimum wage was not enough. Rose had to depend on the food provided by her employers to make ends meet. Savings were a long-lost dream.

All of that was tough, but nothing compared to the treatment by the young waitresses and bus boys. They teased Rose mercilessly about her gait, her age, the way she ate, everything in fact. Laura complained to the chef, who might have realized they could just as easily turn on him as the next senior citizen in the room. He shut the bullies up.

For Laura, Rose was a hidden treasure. Not only did she teach Laura everything about chamber-maiding, and the simple dignity of hard work, but she also taught Laura everything she could about customer service at the inn, which resulted in Laura's getting generous tips for her work. Rose pushed Laura to apply for the job of answering phones during the office night shift—another source of minimum wage income for a couple of hours nightly. It was as if Rose knew that Laura needed to learn about finances early. Which she did.

Lesson: Fear of becoming financially dependent and strafed is a strong motivator.

TEGUCIGALPA

It was Helen's first job after graduate school. About eighteen months into the job, her firm won a contract to conduct a tourism development study for the tourist bureaus of six Central American nations. Helen was asked to do the site reconnaissance, interviews with public and private tourist interests, and evaluate the potentials of local destination resorts and attractions.

Helen was petrified, convinced she wasn't prepared to take on the responsibility of a foreign assignment. She had never really traveled abroad, before, and didn't even know the language. She would be alone except for the counsel of country "controllers"—representatives of each nation's tourist bureau. Would that be enough? Could she do a credible job?

She finally convinced herself to take the assignment and prayed it would be a growing experience. "What could possibly go wrong?" she asked herself.

Under the careful guidance of the six national tourism agencies, she was shown every major guided tour route in Guatemala, El Salvador, Costa Rica, and Nicaragua. Only Honduras and Panama remained to be visited.

She had just left Nicaragua and was a little depressed because the country had not fully recovered from the 1975 earthquake which had leveled its capitol city, Managua. The influence of military rule was strong and onerous in all the countries she visited (except possibly Costa Rica). The oppressive presence of the military was especially heavy in Nicaragua in a futile attempt to protect the largesse of international relief merchandise that had come from overseas. Helen was intensely aware of, and anxious about, the constant military maneuvers as she left Managua for Tegucigalpa, Honduras.

She arrived in the capital city on a Sunday with nothing to do but wait until her agency hosts arrived to escort her on tours of the possible destination sites on Monday. Tegucigalpa was a slow, lethargic city, no doubt due to the summer humidity of a near-jungle existence. By the time Monday morning came, Helen had rested, read, and ate herself into a "south of the border" state of relaxation again.

The agency guide began the tour in a Jeep with cast iron springs. By lunchtime, they had moved into the nation's interior, through the jungles of ever-increasing density and roads that kept getting less paved and more rutted. Her guide was overflowing with his excitement at the opportunity to show Helen the inland, isolated crafts camp located an hour and a half into the dense jungle.

The camp was a complete compound of dorms, mess hall, classrooms, kilns, and showrooms for the hand-hewn ceramic work of the indigenous Honduran population of the area. One instructor had worked for years to establish this "enterprise zone" where members of the community could teach their young the ancient arts, where wholesalers could buy the crafts, and where visitors could watch native crafts being made in the ancient style. Helen's guide took her around to all the market stalls. She was so impressed that she bought the only crafts of her entire visit: a complete set of hand-crafted flatware for four.

It was getting late, and her guide told her that they had to leave to avoid driving the treacherous roads in the dark. After about a twenty-minute drive, a truck came roaring down the road behind them, screeching past the Jeep, making an abrupt halt directly in front of them. The Jeep's driver braked to a stop just in time. Her guide threw his arm in front of Helen to stop her from lurching forward.

Everyone in the Jeep stared as the green curtain covering the back of the truck opened and at least ten soldiers poured out of the back of the vehicle, moving into firing positions with rifles pointed directly at their heads. Another half dozen soldiers hurried out of the front cabin of the truck and positioned themselves closer to the driver and translator, with rifles pointing just inches from their faces.

A commander of the troops began yelling at the driver and her guide; they yelled their answers back. Among the two-way verbal barrage, Helen heard her guide tell her, quickly and almost under his breath, "Don't say anything. Just wait. Stay quiet."

Petrified, Helen stared at the rifle closest to her, looking down its line of sight. So, this was the answer to her question: "What's the worst that can happen?" It will end here, in some anonymous jungle in an exchange that she would never fully comprehend. Would they shoot her? Would they send her body back to her family? Or just to her company? Would they even bother with that?

Slowly, the voices toned down a bit. The armed leader and Helen's guide were the only remaining speakers. Everyone else was listening. The guide spoke more and more, keeping his arm in front of her. Finally, the soldiers lowered their rifles, returned to their truck, and drove off. It was over as quickly as it started.

When the scene became quiet again, her guide explained what had just happened. Another Jeep, looking very much like theirs, had just hit a child in a nearby village and had left the scene of the accident. Everyone was more incensed at the crime than at the prospect of a false arrest.

"You did well," her guide told Helen. "They were young, inexperienced soldiers and very mad. Anything could have happened."

Lesson: Risk is everywhere. Sometimes you know it exists, but you cannot even communicate with it. Sometimes you have to trust others to abate it for you. The only way to avoid all risk is to become isolated and miss out on the journey.

BERESH-TEH

Learning a new language as a kid can be a snap. Learning a new language as an adult takes a bit more effort. Especially if you are also new to the country. Also, if you only have your husband as a teacher . . . after his long work hours. And, if you happen to be newlyweds.

Darla and her husband had just arrived in Iran in August 1975. He was pursuing a new career. They had married the week before they left everything in L.A. and moved to Tehran to start a new life together. He was from there, originally, but after eighteen years away from his homeland, even he had to pause occasionally to remember the right words or phrases in Farsi, the native language of Iran.

To Darla, the language was a lot of squiggly lines and garbled sounds. She hadn't studied a language since undergraduate French, over a decade ago. And Farsi was not French. So, here she was in Tehran with her two year old master's degree, no job anymore, and no prospect for a job unless she could at least make a dent in that language.

They lived in Tehran's only high-rise apartment building—near the top of the fifteen-story structure, in a tiny one-bedroom with an even tinier kitchen. He would come home from a long day at work and try to help her start learning a few words here and there. She would come home from an even longer day of doing nothing, but maybe reading in the living room or trying to make sense out of the strange sounds that seemed even sillier when they came out of her mouth.

For excitement, in the evening, they'd take the elevator down to the basement level of the building and shop at the mini-mart there. Since the apartment building was oriented to foreign businessmen on temporary assignment in Tehran, the inventory was strong on canned goods. One major supplier of the canned equivalent of "Mama's Own Persian Home Cookin'" was the company Yek-O-Yek, which was translated into "one-o-one." For a can of food, you do *not* want to hear anything about "yeck," but at least it helped Darla to start learning the numbers.

"*Yek*"—one. "*Doh*"—two. "*Seh*"—three. "*Cha-Har*"—four. "*Panj*"—five. "*Sheesh*"! No, really! Six is "*sheesh*." Darla chuckled a lot in the early sessions on numbers.

The mini-mart was pretty safe territory: everyone was a foreigner, although the proprietor tended to stare at Darla—the blonde-haired, pasty-white-skinned female in obviously California garb.

The real stares came when they ventured out for a walk on the streets, say, to buy a sheet of fresh Persian bread from the nearby bakery. Darla learned the bakery was called a "*noon-vai*"—meaning the fabrication place (vai) for bread (noon). She learned that bread was written as "*nan*," but pronounced as "noon" in Tehran. Oh, great—two dictionaries to learn—one written, one spoken! Maybe there would be even more dialects when they visited other places. Sheesh! (And she *didn't* mean "six"!)

At the noon-vai, he would get into line and everyone would stare at Darla standing beside him. "Oh, well, get used to it—smile," she'd say to herself. When his turn came, he'd always order his bread saying the same thing. To Darla, it sounded like, "$(*)&)(* bszh t. bzzz-mttt!"

When they returned to the apartment, she asked him to explain to her what he just said. He had to think before he could remember.

"Was it '*yeh-doo-neh*'?" he asked. "That means, 'one of those.'"

Darla told him he said something else that sounded more like a buzz-saw cutting through wood.

"Was it '*bee-zah-matt*'?" he asked. "That means 'please.'"

"Right! But that was just at the end. There was more buzzing in between," she explained.

"Oh, you mean '*beresh-teh*,'" he said.

"Yes! What's that mean?" she asked.

"'Beresh-teh' is like 'well done' for bread. It means a loaf with some charring on both sides from the hot flames of the open oven. So, altogether, I probably said to the baker, "'Yeh-doo-neh, beresh-teh, bee-zah-matt.' That would mean 'one of those, well done, please.'"

So, finally, Darla's tongue and brain had something they could play with in the back of her mind. During the next visit to the noon-vai, she listened more carefully as he and the others ordered "yek," "yeh-doo-neh," "doh-ta," or "seh-ta," pieces of bread. Then she recognized "please" ("bee-zah-matt") and "thank you" ("*merci*"—hey, something familiar at last!)

She asked him later about "merci"—why would Iranians switch to French? He described how several French words had been adopted into Farsi, but explained that the proper Farsi term for "thank you" (nice and polite and all) was the tongue-twister: "*mot-schak-eram*," meaning, "I'm really grateful" or "I'm thankful."

Darla had a lot of new words and sounds to play with plus the start of some concepts. That was a beginning. It wasn't much later that he called from work and said he'd be later than usual. "Fine," Darla thought to herself, "I'm really, really busy reading." Then, while refilling her Orange Crush, she saw that all the bread in the kitchen was gone and that he'd be home too late for the two of them to do to a bread run. She decided, "It's now or never!"

Darla checked to see if she had the four coins he usually spent for bread, threw on a jacket, braved all the stares as the lone blonde Western female in the elevator to the lobby, walked out to the sidewalk, around the corner, up the street a few blocks. The line at the noon-vai was a bit longer than usual—it was the prime pre-dinner time. She stood at the end of the line, towering by at least a foot over the children and older women in front of her (and soon, behind her).The line progressed and, as each buyer left the baker, he or she would sneak one last stare and chuckle.

Darla was sure her cheeks were magenta by the time she stepped into the bakery—with just one short lady making her purchase before her. The chit-chat between her and the seller was a bit longer than Darla was used to, but ultimately it was her turn, and he (very kindly) looked at her with a smile and asked, "Yes, ma'am?"

But Darla was committed. She couldn't even *understand* English anymore. All she knew were the words she'd been rehearsing ever since she'd left the apartment. Like a soldier, reporting name, rank, and serial number, she said, "Yeh-doo-neh, beresh-teh, bee-zah-matt!"

And the place went silent. Except for the baker who reached down, found a really, really perfect sheaf of bread and brought it up for her approval.

"Okay?" he asked.

"Mot-schak-eram," Darla replied and handed him the coins, praying to both their Gods that the price had not changed since their last visit. He wrapped the bread in a page of the newspaper (hey—the bread's already been charred in the open fire, so what's the difference?), then took the coins, nodded to Darla with a big grin and said something that she made a mental note to ask her husband about if she ever made it home again.

Darla walked back out of the bakery and saw just a hint of wonderment in the eyes of those in line.

"I *did* it!" she said to herself and beamed all the way back home.

Lesson: It doesn't really matter what you know until you have the courage to test it by the hot fires outside of yourself. Out there—you could just as easily be ridiculed as admired. Taking that first uncertain step makes the adrenalin surge and lifts you to some grand new height from which you will never again return to the place or the person you were before.

END OF ONE CAREER

Sue finished graduate school in 1973 with a specialization in urban land economics, which meant she could make a contribution as an economist (someone who knows about how to manage with scarce resources) or as someone who knew something about the real estate marketplace. After working as an economist for planning firms, she and her husband moved overseas in 1975. And that's when Sue learned a major lesson in career planning.

They moved to Iran, where oil was coming out of the earth at $22 a barrel—a pocket-book-burning rate at the time. Money was being thrown at any kind of project throughout Iran: good, bad, or worse. In that economy, the prevailing wage or demand for someone with a unique ability to deal with shortages was at or close to zero. Sue's best laid plans for a sensible, long-term, viable, professional career, based on the two pillars of real estate and economics, simply collapsed.

Many recent graduates in the twenty-first century post-financial-meltdown economy find themselves in similar straits right here in America, that bastion of capitalism. Middle managers have been booted outside the corporate hierarchy to make room for lower-cost labor or non-labor options. They face the same challenge that Sue faced back in the mid-1970s. Defense industry and aerospace engineers know what it's like to have been priced out of today's competitive global economy.

In Iran in 1975, Sue did what any red-blooded unemployed American would do: she begged for work. She changed her profession to "what work do you need done?" She read, wrote, did whatever needed doing. She reorganized corporate libraries. Started libraries. Moved cases. Wrote cases. Wrote articles. Read books. She did whatever she could do, just to be working.

Reality Number Three came in 1978 when Sue and her spouse were relocated by his employer to Greece where, by law, she was not allowed to work in deference to the Greek unemployed. Her husband, as an "importer" of new jobs, was more than welcome to work, but Sue would be considered taking food from some Greek breadwinner's table if she contracted to make a contribution in return for compensation.

What do you do when your careers are gone and you are forbidden by the state from earning an income? You can either study or donate your labors. Sue did both.

About that time, there were rumblings around this thing called "a personal computer." A few magazines had cropped up at the local Greek kiosks. Sue bought every issue she could lay her hands on. This was not light bedtime reading, either—especially for someone with a liberal arts background. Bits and bytes and accumulator registers required some serious concentration.

Sue and her husband were staying in a small one-room studio. Into this tiny living-room-plus-bedroom, she added a study hall. She divided the mornings and afternoons into six one-hour segments with an hour's break for lunch and errands. Each day, she set out her day's self-study "classes": flow charting, BASIC language, specific program debugging, general book reading, magazine reading, and problem sets.

This continued for about two months until she decided she needed to know more about who was making these personal computers. Sue needed more information from the makers, the vendors as they were called. Since Greece was an international business hub, the American embassy was able to give her the addresses of major global computer manufacturers with headquarter offices in Athens.

But personal computers in 1979 were being made by companies like Altair, PET, Apple, and other names nobody really knew. They were not yet being made by IBM, Digital, or Prime. Sue couldn't believe someone in those companies wasn't working on it. So, she went and asked them about it. "What are you doing to address the personal computer marketplace?" Sue asked as if she were an international correspondent from *Byte Magazine*—London office—on temporary assignment to Athens.

Next, her sabbatical curriculum added on-site company interviews scheduled each morning. After two weeks of frustration, she began to believe the Athens market was untapped by the microcomputer industry. She received brusque brush-offs by some firms and hard-sell sales tactics from others. Then, she finally hit pay dirt.

A Greek manager at Prime actually invited her into his office where they talked about what they both had only read about in personal or microcomputer magazines. He had an uncle who had bought a Tandy Model I and brought it back with him when he retired to Greece after years as an IBM vacuum tube repair engineer. The manager took Sue's name and phone number, saying he'd talk to his uncle about her interest and get back to her.

Sue floated on the bus ride back to the apartment. She beamed at everyone she met in the lobby. She was bursting at the seams when she reported her success to her husband that evening. Then came the wait. One week, two weeks, no call. Finally his call broke her short-term depression. His uncle had agreed to see her one evening next week.

Sue and her husband went together to meet him and his family in a northern suburb. The retired engineer brought out piles of old personal computer magazines and books that he'd collected since the first *Popular Electronics* issue announced the arrival of the micro-computer revolution. He told them his story as an electronics engineer. Finally, he showed Sue his Tandy Model I. It was downstairs in the cellar, in a room all by itself except for the washing machine and dryer and a whole lot of cables. He agreed to loan her some of his magazines. Before parting, they agreed to exchange time on his Model I for her typing programs into the computer that he found in those magazines.

Sue read every issue, book, and line of code she could find in his collection. She taught herself how the BASIC language worked in real programs by testing lines of code from the "how to" articles. She learned how to visualize the progression of a program using flow charts just as she once had diagrammed sentences. She typed in and debugged the programs that he wanted to play by running them again and again and again—sometimes even finding errors that the authors had not yet discovered.

For the next several weeks, Sue's husband would drop her off at nine in the morning and would have to tear her away from the keyboard at noon, two to three days a week.

"Just one more line of code—it'll take just a second."

For the rest of the year, Sue learned by doing almost as much as she learned by reading.

Lesson: A profession is something that you are proud to be doing. A career is the ability to take your skills and knowledge and apply them in any venue, any venture. It involves associating with people whom you respect, who have much to teach you and to share with you. A career is something that is so much fun that you don't want to stop doing it . . . ever.

DEFERRING ENJOYMENT

Christine was advancing, professionally, in her company and her career. She loved her work and consistently got great annual performance reviews. The company had an array of corporate training programs. Christine signed up for all of them and even was invited to teach a few. She loved learning.

There was only one woman in leadership at the firm, or at least only one in Christine's area of software engineering. Sue had been with the company for years, having come to the firm through an early merger/acquisition of Sue's family-owned company. Sue supported legacy systems until they died out in the competition from newer third- or fourth-generation applications. Sue survived and made it to the head of a major department. Christine wanted to learn from Sue—especially what it might take for Christine herself, to take on more leadership roles. Christine mustered the courage to talk with Sue after a departmental meeting. Would Sue be interested in having coffee someday? Sue seemed flattered by the attention, and they agreed on a day.

When they got together the following week, Christine didn't sense the same warmth as she felt at the department meeting. Their conversation was light—Sue talked about her cats, Christine talked about her latest class. Sue mentioned how much the company had changed over the years. Her biggest challenge, lately, was keeping the weekly change control meetings from regressing into total war between software, network, and application development department heads. Christine said she admired how well Sue kept the meetings focused on the subject and moved issues towards resolution. Christine asked for suggestions about how she might learn to be as effective as Sue and grow in her job.

Sue said, "Well, I suppose everyone needs to gather together a good collection of management advice books for her personal library." Then they shared a few thoughts about books they'd read recently.

Sue finally opened up and said, "Do you want to know what I'd really like to do with my career? I'd like to retire and take ocean cruises to all corners of the world."

That was not exactly what Christine had hoped to hear by way of career advice. No career plan. No personal growth ambitions. No leadership strategy. No aspirations other than to toss it all, lean back, and sail away. To be as respectful as possible, Christine encouraged her to talk further about her plans, even though Christine was frustrated that this woman, whom she admired so much for her endurance, was just waiting for her exit papers.

Christine tried to coax her back to the idea of growth within the firm, but Sue expressed no sense of, or interest in, the subject. Sue was not the career role model that Christine had hoped to find. Later on, Christine thought about the discussion and wondered if Sue might have been holding back to keep Christine from competing for her job. Christine decided to take Sue at face value and not ascribe to her any ulterior motives. Sue was who she was because of her experience.

Christine searched for something of substance she might take from this encounter. Sue's longing for deferred enjoyment—only after retirement—persuaded Christine to consider ways that she could keep the excitement of learning and her enjoyment of the job alive while still with the company. She would find ways to take those cruises along the way, while she could still enjoy them and benefit from the experience.

Lesson: Role models can be the people who show you what not to do.

JULIA BLOOMFIELD*

Many people have affected the shape of Frances's life but the one who looms largest is a woman who fundamentally changed its direction.

Her name is Julia Bloomfield. Frances met her twenty-seven years ago, just after taking a position as assistant editor at a magazine in London called *The Architectural Review*. Frances had barely started the job when the editor-in-chief threw her into the proverbial deep end, demanding that she produce a special issue on "Young America"—sixty pages of editorial to be ready within a matter of weeks.

---

*Written and contributed by Frances Anderton, Host and Executive Producer, KCRW's DnA: Design and Architecture (kcrw.com/dna).

Frances's sum total of prior experience with the United States was two weeks' vacation in New York. Frankly, she was stumped. Where to start?

She turned to an old professor who happened to have lived in the US, and he said simply, "Call Julia Bloomfield."

Julia, it turned out, was an expat Brit who had moved to New York in the 1970s and had become editor of an architecture publication there. Now, in 1987, she had been hired away by the Getty Research Institute to be their head of publications and had recently moved to Los Angeles.

Frances found a number and called, and a warm if imperious sounding lady answered the phone. She gingerly explained why she was calling. Julia responded immediately with, "Forget young America, you need to focus on LA. Come and stay with me, and I'll help."

"LA has become a hotbed of experimental architecture by emerging talent like Frank Gehry, Thom Mayne and Eric Owen Moss," Julia said, easily rattling off prominent names in the field. She offered to introduce Frances around and invited her to come stay in her new home in Santa Monica.

Up to that point, there had been no plans for Frances to go anywhere; she was supposed to put together the issue based on research by phone in London. But the editor agreed, so within a matter of days, she was on the plane to LA and, on landing, took a taxi to Julia's home in Santa Monica.

A tall, regal-looking woman with straw blonde hair greeted Frances at the entry gate. The two immediately sat down and started chatting.

Despite her years in the United States, Julia still sounded like a member of British royalty (her father was high up at the Bank of England). She had a hearty laugh and a naughty sense of humor, with regular diversions into reenactments of scenes from Peter Sellers movies. But she always came back to seriousness, focusing with laser acuity on the project at hand, making notes, calling people, advising which topics to cover. Within a short space of time, Frances felt totally at home with this person, and inspired by her.

The special issue on Los Angeles proved a success, and Frances had become smitten with both the city and Julia's friendship. In meeting Julia, Frances had found a kindred spirit: a Brit who loved America, who had channeled her passion for architecture into publishing and editing, loved good writing and could spot a typo from a mile off.

They stayed in touch over the years—with postcards and visits—until, four years later, Frances moved to Los Angeles to edit a small architecture newspaper for the American Institute of Architects.

Again Julia was part of the story.

Frances lived with Julia when she first arrived in Los Angeles, and her friend was a constant presence through all the tricky first experiences of a newcomer—from helping Frances secure a car to giving guidance on American English, to supporting her ambitions for the newspaper.

They found increasingly that they were both similar and complementary—sharing interests but different expressions of them. Julia was a perfectionist and classic in her tastes, resistant to the quirky, loose, inventive spirit of LA that Frances fully embraced and celebrated and encouraged her mentor to enjoy.

After six months, it was time for Frances to find her own home. Once again, Julia enabled a defining change in Frances's life.

One day Julia's friend Frank Gehry, came for lunch, and Frances mentioned she was looking for an apartment. "Oh," he said, "I have a building you can live in."

Within a matter of weeks, Frances moved into an apartment building Gehry had co-designed with a colleague in the early 1960s. Frances still lives there today.

As time passed, the relationship became mutual. Even though Julia is older, Frances was able to be a support to Julia in return. Behind Julia's capable demeanor lay anxieties and challenges.

And whenever either of them felt down or somehow inadequate to the tasks at work or home, each has served as the other's confidence booster.

Had Julia responded differently to that call from a total stranger in London, Frances's life would have taken a very different path. Because of Julia, Frances moved to LA, found rewarding work in journalism and communications, and discovered the place she has called home for twenty-three years.

Frances considers herself extremely lucky to have found such a mentor.

"Thank you Julia Bloomfield."

Lesson: Mentors can present themselves at the most unexpected times and places.

HOW WE DO BUSINESS

Women need to ask themselves, "how are we conducting business?" Are we acting professionally or are we simply extending our home life and lifestyles into the business environment?

Tori said she tries to deliver more business to women entrepreneurs who have earned it. One example was her decision to use the Chair Massage while waiting for her car to be serviced. Tori admired the young lady's marketing creativity: contracting with the larger firm to position herself and her business at a high-traffic location where customers might have time, money, and a proclivity to purchase her services. Good business decisions earn customers' attention.

Tori said she also has given business to website developers, editors, lawyers, and accountants—all of the female persuasion. When they deliver the goods—according to their agreements or understanding—it's a positive business experience.

But, when Tori gets stalled and put off or ignored for days on end by a woman business person who puts her business clients low on her priorities, then Tori get concerned. That's when the proverbial rubber meets the road. That is the test of a true business person—female or male.

Tori said she does not like to hear the litany of excuses about a woman business person who needed to go shopping for the kids going back to school. Tori did not want to hear about all of the other clients or commitments that the woman chose to place ahead of her requirements. Nor was Tori interested in hearing about the woman business person's "work-family balancing act" because—as sure as anything—that woman was not interested in hearing about the host of challenges that Tori was addressing, silently and successfully.

Tori was frustrated when she would arrange educational or training events in her area of expertise, invite friends and associates to participate, but would get more emails from women "explaining why they could not attend" because their calendars were over-committed. Why would Tori care about no-shows?

Or perhaps the woman business person was a public employee, charged with approving Tori's license or contract or service request. Why would she believe Tori might be interested in hearing her litany of:

- the backlog of unaddressed business decisions she has failed to process;
- the layers of administrative incompetence which she accepts as her workplace; or
- all of the causes and cases for which she is responsible?

Just because she is a business woman does not mean that others—who also are attempting to get their job done—have any desire to listen to or to share her Soap Opera, her Tale of Woe, Her Share of Misery.

Nike just came out with a new ad campaign which they say is "just for women." The new slogan is: "Here I Am!" It is supposed to help women boost their egos as a first step toward heightening their willingness to compete.

Lesson: Perhaps more women in business should listen to Nike's older and wiser slogan, "Just Do It!"

OVERCOMING FEAR

Mandy hated the thought of public speaking. Hate wasn't the correct term—more like loathed, detested, despised, and most of all feared the idea of standing before groups of more than two people and talking with any coherence. The suggestion put beads of sweat on her forehead, tremors in her knees, and constrictions in her throat.

But, here she was, co-owner of a business enterprise, ready to go after funding and expected to appear before bankers, lenders, angel and venture capitalists. Mandy could no longer pass the responsibility for the business pitch to her partner, Stan. She had to up her game and overcome this phobia if they were to take the company to its next logical level.

She and Stan decided to go cold turkey and pitch the business plan in a small local venture competition. The event was sold to entrepreneurs as an easy introduction to accelerating your business and preparing owners for the challenges of talking with investors. Mandy and Stan signed up. They agreed that he would test the waters first, and she'd learn by observation.

They worked for days on their slide deck—the PowerPoint presentation slides that accompanied their pitch. They refined and retuned Stan's pitch to get it under the required ten minutes.

The big day came, and they hoped they were ready. The event started with a presentation coach giving a mini-course on "How to Pitch." Stan and Mandy looked at each other with new trepidation, thinking "NOW they tell us this, after we've set ourselves out on our course." The instructor recognized the looks of fear in everyone's eyes and said, "Don't change anything, now. Stay the course and learn from the experience."

When Stan's turn came, he did just that—stayed with his script. Mandy thought he did well. The five judges, venture and angel capital investors, were kind, but had a lot of suggestions to improve the presentation. Stan was in such a state that he couldn't remember all their advice. He could only hope Mandy was taking great notes.

Afterwards, Mandy talked with Andrea, the only woman judge, about Stan's presentation. Andrea asked Mandy why she didn't present. "I'm interested, but petrified," Mandy replied. "I thought Stan did really well, but he and I seem to be the only people in the room who thought so."

Andrea laughed and told Mandy she liked their business concept and saw a lot of potential. They talked about working together over the next couple of weeks to prepare Mandy to hone her own presentation. As a business advisor, Andrea had developed a strategy to enable entrepreneurs to fine-tune their pitch for angel and venture capital audiences.

They began with Mandy giving her presentation, including her PowerPoint slide deck, in front of a video camera. They reviewed the recording together. Andrea analyzed the presentation like a director trying to improve an actor's performance—little criticism, but lots of pointing to what Mandy did well or to something that distracted from her presentation. Mandy was surprised at her reaction to the video—it wasn't really as bad as she's expected. Now she could see what the audience was seeing—the bad habits she needed to correct.

Andrea asked Mandy to tell her about a woman she admired. Mandy described her grandmother with genuine affection, how she was unique for her generation—strong, caring, and a woman in business herself. Andrea said to think of her grandmother in the audience and imagine how proud she would be to hear her granddaughter talking so confidently about her business.

Andrea showed a slide deck that demonstrated some of the essential items that investors would expect from an entrepreneur's presentation. They walked through each slide and discussed everything from the font size, the color and background, the number of words, and the flow of the message. "You're telling a story," Andrea said. "You're trying to capture their attention, keep them interested, and carry them on to the very end of your message. And, you are trying to convince them that you are worth the risk of investing." They talked through the items that Mandy and Stan had not covered in their presentation and how they could incorporate those important topics, while letting go of some less important slides.

Mandy described some of the highlights she captured. "I realized that a pitch is presenting the facts that the audience wants to hear, not the story that I want to tell them. That was a major change. Also, I learned that a few well-designed graphics could be far more effective in conveying a concept. Too many words on a slide take a lot of time to explain and force the audience to read rather than listen to what you're saying."

Andrea put the burden back on Mandy. "You need to practice, at home, in front of a mirror or your roommate. You need to construct a few sentences appropriate to each slide, but make every sentence count. Shorter sentences will let you deliver a more powerful message. Every morning, for the next week, talk through your slide deck until you know with confidence exactly what you need to say. Then, just imagine your grandmother sitting in the back of the room, smiling!"

Lesson: Replace fear with the certainty and confidence in your own knowledge and capabilities. There is no magic to overcoming the prospect or risk of failure. If you can imagine success in your own mind, can action and success be very far away?

ACCIDENTAL MENTORSHIP

Stacy attended a panel of women in leadership where four women were speaking about their experiences being selected to serve on public company boards of directors. The inevitable question came from the audience, "Did you mentor others on your way to the top?" The implication of the question, inevitably, was "Where do I find someone like you to mentor me?"

The answer from one of the panelists both surprised and impressed Stacy because she knew the woman and the story of her career, having interviewed her for an article in a prominent business magazine not long before.

The woman panelist said, "I don't think I *intentionally* mentored anyone. However, throughout my career—whenever and wherever I was given any opportunity for advancement—I tried to choose the best talent possible to work with me in that situation. It just happened that a lot of very competent women fit that search criteria."

Stacy knew a great deal about the woman's background and experience from the research for her article. Stacy observed that there were many pathways where that individual consistently worked to make things better: from academia, nonprofit, and entrepreneurial to corporate venues. The woman in leadership did receive both honors and recognition for the many enhancements, improvements, positive change, and remedies to problems from which others too often simply shied away.

The point the panelist emphasized was that she did not stop and hand-hold a few prospective individuals in some artificial program along the way. What she did was create a very wide swath of opportunity throughout her entire professional journey. She didn't help a handful of ambitious young women. She helped literally thousands of women of all ages in all walks of life through her work.

Lesson: Effortless mentorship—that is the role model and mentor we might strive to emulate.

THE SHEPHERD BOY

Leslie had survived the dot-com bubble, the financial crash, and the latest recession all before they finally moved her cheese. Her job was outsourced, right-sized, downsized, eliminated, transitioned, and kaput.

She'd been thinking of a change, but they beat her to it. "Nothing personal," her boss had said. "We just don't need that department anymore." Right. "Nothing personal." The severance was good. The transitional support services were predictable: representatives from a management consulting firm would meet with her, review her resume, and help her find "another job in the same industry."

Leslie didn't really think that that was her best choice. Taking "just another job" probably would lead to "just another" job elimination in maybe two to three years. The writing was pretty much on the wall for that type of work in that type of company. Leslie didn't really want to look at the prospect of doing the same thing in just another cubicle until someone else decided to do some "not personal" to her again.

Leslie had a lot of experience in her field, a generous quantity of credentials, knew a lot of software products, and had some very creative and potentially innovative ideas about new applications that could satisfy customer needs. Her strong suit had been a close understanding of what the company's customers wanted and needed. The company hadn't always listened to her feedback and, therefore, had not grown their customer and revenue base as much as Leslie believed they could.

While considering the management consultant's "program" to re-fit her for the same old job, Leslie fondly remembered spending summers with her Aunt Betty in Chicago who had broken barriers and stereotypes in the 1950s by starting her own business—first as a seamstress, but then as a clothes designer of top fashions for wedding parties. Leslie remembered Aunt Betty's favorite story from the old country.

A shepherd boy was charged with tending his master's herd of sheep. For years, the boy mindfully protected the sheep against nature's elements, wolves, and the like.

One day, a robber came, grabbed one of the sheep, and started to run away with it. The master yelled at the boy to go catch the thief and bring the lamb back to its owner. The boy began the chase but, as he came within yards of catching the robber, he suddenly stopped in his tracks. Then he turned and walked back to the master.

"Why did you stop?" the master yelled at the boy. "You almost caught him!"

"I suddenly realized that he was running for himself, while I was running for you," the shepherd boy replied.

With that, he tossed his shepherd's crook at the feet of the master and left to find his own way.

Aunt Betty said that she could always sew clothing for the family, and probably always would. But, there was something special about being in charge of her own fortunes and destiny as owner of her own shop with her own customers. It gave her a sense of great pride in her work and her ability to earn her own living.

Taking a lesson from her aunt, while her colleagues signed up with the management consulting firm for help in re-writing their resume, Leslie took the road less traveled and hunted for some entrepreneurial business advisory services. She found savvy, experienced advisors at the Senior Corps of Retired Executives (SCORE). She found classes and technical assistance on writing a business plan from the Small Business Development Corporation (SBDC). She found peer entrepreneurs at the Women's Economic Development Corp. (WEDC) and resources at the National Association of Women Business Owners (NAWBO). She signed up for Toastmasters to learn how to present her ideas more effectively.

She started her own business developing a software service that she'd discovered was needed and valued by her former customers. She hired a programmer to help her design and build the product, incorporated the company, built a sales team, brought on a few key customers and began to establish a reputation as a businesswoman providing new and innovative services that her former managers had told her would never succeed. "Nothing personal."

Within two years, her former company was acquired in a hostile takeover that essentially erased all evidence that the firm ever existed. In three years, Leslie's own firm was revenue positive. In five years, she was hiring her fifth employee. As she shook the hand of the newest person to join her firm, Leslie said to her, "My hope is that the most frustrating day that you spend here with us at this firm is STILL better and more satisfying than the best day you might have spent working for any other company."

Lesson: Empowerment is what happens when an individual realizes she or he has a choice: to serve other masters or to serve one's own priority interests. To leave behind the servitude mentality—the idea that we should be serving and helping everyone else—elevates our thinking and our potential.

TALENT SEARCH

Alicia had an impressive legal career, capped by her nomination to one of the more important sections of the local bar association, where she had the opportunity to showcase her expertise in the section's legal domain and work with other lawyers to review, propose, and finalize recommendations that went all the way to the national agenda of the American Bar Association.

Throughout her career, Alicia had worked with up-and-coming women lawyers and ensured they were presented with challenging work opportunities that would help them advance in their chosen field. She had promoted women in the firm to positions of leadership when and as they clearly earned the advancement and recognition. She counseled them when it was clear the prospect aspired to a partnership position.

Alicia was named to a professional association that recognized both the career and community service aspects of her career. She rose quickly in their ranks and was named to their board of directors of the nonprofit. She served first as vice president of programs, then vice president of membership, and ultimately president of the organization and chair of the board. At each level, Alicia made improvements and enhancements, reaching out into the organization's constituency to tap the shoulder of new speaker prospects or new members who reflected the best and the brightest of the profession and the community itself. Panelists whom she brought to their group's events gave new insight and perspective, both men and women in the profession. New members whom she persuaded to join likewise were individuals that added to the stature of the association.

Having worked hard over the years from the inside of corporations and organizations, Alicia knew well what it took to add value, make quality contributions, and to rise to positions of leadership. She always was on the lookout for new talent to work on projects and committees. But, Alicia discovered that, as she rose in the association, the harder she had to search to find executive talent. The toughest challenge was to find women who were "ready, willing, and able" to serve.

Alicia developed a speakers' bureau for the association, but needed both volunteer speakers and individuals to serve on committees chartered to coordinate, schedule, and promote the program. Repeatedly, women committee members promised to take on a task but dropped the ball. She was disappointed when a prominent woman speaker was scheduled to make a presentation, but failed to show—without explanation.

For a while, Alicia thought it might be her leadership style that could be causing the fall-off of support and involvement by women whom she considered natural choices for the association's leadership roles. Then, the organization prepared to elect a new president and, as it always had done in the past, the sitting president asked the vice president to accept the nomination for the next two years as head of the entity. She, the vice president, declined, leaving the board surprised and astounded that she would step away from this leadership opportunity.

Alicia took her concerns to Joan, a fellow board member and a lawyer in the real estate field. Joan's experience echoed Alicia's. Joan said she also saw a fall-off of women in leadership ranks at commercial real estate firms—especially at the point where women opted to stay at salary levels rather than step up to positions where commissions determined compensation. Joan suggested that those women who decide to take on the commission levels of work were more willing to accept that level of uncertainty in exchange for the potentially higher returns. The same might be true, she hypothesized, about women deciding to stay at the lower profile support roles in the association rather than take on the uncertain challenges of committee or board responsibilities. That certainly didn't explain everything, but the end result contributed to the problem.

Alicia was torn. She didn't see it as her responsibility to bring the subject up at board or committee meetings. Everybody there could see the same things happening that Alicia observed. She had to assume the women members of the organization had their reasons for their decisions, but none of them came to her and none of them offered any explanation for their choices. Her reputation was on the line, so Alicia became much more cautious about her talent search choices.

Lesson: Finding talented individuals to mentor is a challenge faced by women and men alike. For successful mentoring to take place, both the mentor and mentee need to be on the same page, with similar or at least consistent priorities. Sometimes it's difficult to find talented individuals who will leave the certainty of their current status to take on the risks and opportunities of leadership.

WHOM DO YOU ADMIRE?

Ursula likes to say, "Tell me whom you admire among today's women in business or among contemporary women in leadership. What you tell me about them will tell me a great deal about you."

Ursula admires women who are greater or better than she is (today) because she aspires to improve. She is interested in women of achievement who present role models about the individual she might one day become. Women of a lesser level, who present no threat, who sacrifice themselves by giving away everything of themselves until there is nothing left but a memory, these women are not the role models Ursula chooses.

When she sees successful women, Ursula asks herself what makes them successful? What decisions did they make? What investments did they make in themselves. She does not chip away at women of achievement, knocking them off some artificial pedestal. She stands on the foundation of her own strong self-esteem, looking at achievement as training and education for herself.

Ursula is capable of analyzing the lives of successful women. She looks for more information from the likes of Christine Amanpour, Laura Logan, and Soledad O'Brien than she does about "conversations" from Katie Couric, Barbara Walters, or Oprah Winfrey.

"Give me a woman of achievement, any day, over a woman who is obviously less than myself. At least I know how hard a journey it has been for me to achieve, today, that to which I might lay claim. I may not be a peer to the more successful women in business, but I do know that at least I have met the challenge of the few very good women who encouraged me to try harder, to reach further, to dare even more than they did. I will cheer their achievements just as my brothers cheered their role models: with unabashed joy and enthusiasm."

Lesson: If we have role models ahead of us in this great race, then we know there exist opportunities not only to improve but also for the next generation to succeed. That is what stirs our own minds and spirit to reach for the stars.

INDRA NOOYI

In the June 2008 issue of *The Costco Connection*,[2] the discount retailer's quarterly magazine, Richard Deitsch interviewed the president/CEO of PepsiCo, Indra Nooyi, and showed a lot more respect for her achievements and business perspectives and a lot less appeal to prurient interests than was the case in interviews with Porfolio.com (Conde Nast), *Fortune* magazine or *The Wall Street Journal*.

For the Costco interview, Ms. Nooyi was not posed to maximize the exposure of her breasts, legs or, thighs as is typical of most mainstream media publications. Ms. Nooyi spoke intelligently about PepsiCo's core leadership values: "Performance with Purpose." Finally, Ms. Nooyi showed the good grace and decency to be "visibly uncomfortable" with premature praise, admitting that it was—as yet—too soon to measure her success. She is ready and willing to be tested on her merits.

"I am just getting my feet wet. I am earning my stripes. I want those stripes to be bright. I want them screaming. Then you can write about me."

What you learn from *The Costco Connection* article are Indra Nooyi's "Five C's to Success."

Competence: "You can't move up in any job or in life unless you are damn good at something."

Courage and confidence: "if you are not willing to break some china in speaking up, when you think something is not being done right, what is the value of having all that competency?"

Communication: "If you can't communicate what you are going to do in a compelling way, that is a wasted thing."

Compass: "If you don't have moral integrity, it is all for naught."

Coaching: "Mentors find you. You don't find them. A mentor has picked you because you have the competence, the courage and confidence, you are a great communicator and you have a moral compass. They say, 'I want to hitch my horse to yours because I think you are going to go places and you will take me with you. Not because I need it, but because I like the ride.'"

Lesson: It is not necessary for outstanding women to stop doing their job and reach out to others who would aspire to succeed and follow in their footsteps. By their own words and deeds, outstanding women create life and career case studies from which we may learn powerful lessons.

JOLINE GODFREY

Today, Joline Godfrey calls herself "an innovator in family financial education." She is the authority on "raising financially fit kids" through her firm, Independent Means Inc. (IMI), ". . . the leading provider of financial education for children and families. Since 1992, IMI has created and successfully delivered financial education experiences for more than 100,000 kids and 10,000 parents worldwide."[3]

Ms. Godfrey grew up in a small town in rural Maine and graduated with a BS in Child Development from the University of Maine in 1972. She went on to earn an MSW from Boston University's School of Social Work. She worked as a clinical social counselor, providing family and therapeutic services to officers and employees at the Polaroid Corp. She was an executive at Polaroid for ten years, a career documented by two Harvard Business School case studies describing how she developed a service-oriented business project within the firm, and then spun that business off as Odysseum Inc., her own company, providing international learning design services for Fortune 500 clients. She sold that company in 1990.[4]

Ms. Godfrey was named the McGraw-Hill Intrapreneur of the Year in 1987 and was selected by the Kellogg Foundation as a Kellogg fellow in 1989. She was awarded an honorary degree in business from Bentley College in 1995.

In 1992, she and New York–based television producer, Jane Lytle, collected and distributed 250,000 books to Libros para Chile, a gift to help revitalize Chile's public libraries after years of neglect by the Pinochet regime. The program was a project managed as part of her Kellogg National Leadership Fellowship; a joint collaboration between Ms. Godfrey's nonprofit foundation, the Knowledge Network, and the National Library of Chile.

Ms. Godfrey is the author of five books on financial literacy and financial advice for parents, families, and women. In her first book, *No More Frogs to Kiss*,[5] Ms. Godfrey described how twenty-two women came together in 1993 on a retreat for members of the group, An Income of Her Own, to discuss ways to "give economic power to the next generation."

An Income of Her Own (AIOHO) was a California-based not-for-profit organization created by Ms. Godfrey and Karen Schafer to encourage teenage girls to consider business ownership. AIOHO sponsored an annual business plan competition for young women and an annual conference held in collaboration with the American Woman's Economic Development Corp. Other products and services designed to increase young women's skills and economic literacy included a summer entrepreneurship camp, a newsletter, and a board game that rewarded players for making entrepreneurial choices.

By 1996, Ms. Godfrey had transformed An Income of Her Own into the gender neutral for-profit enterprise Independent Means Inc. based in Santa Barbara, California, serving families around the world. That shift was the result of a growing awareness that, in the early to mid-nineties, financial education for girls was still an idea ahead of its time. It was during those years that Take Our Daughters to Work Day, a much less radical idea, caused such controversy. Godfrey realized she would need to continue her quest for girls' economic empowerment in new ways that would engage parents and policy makers rather than enrage them. That approach, embodied in the Independent Means methods and content, includes gender neutral financial education that is experiential, engaging, and fun. Camp Start-Up, which celebrates its twentieth year of operation in 2014, generally enjoys a 50/50 split of male and female teens.

No More Frogs to Kiss is "the essential handbook for arming the next generation of women with the knowledge and experience they need to ensure their economic independence. [It] presents 99 entertaining 'action plans' to teach girls how to become financially empowered . . . learn to find deals in the marketplace, use business vocabulary intelligently, start a small home business more profitable (and fun) than baby-sitting and develop the habit of saving for the future. Accompanying each activity are provocative statistics about women and money, as well as stories of girls and women who have succeeded in their own business ventures."[6]

In the foreword, Gloria Steinem described the origin of the book's title, taken from the many myths that were told to young princesses of those days:

"If she would just . . . kiss the right frog, she was told, all would turn out well. She would be rich, beautiful, and well cared for by the man of her dreams."

"That is the amazing thing about myths. They are so powerful that we internalize them even when they contradict our deepest experience . . . But then, this is what myths are for: to safeguard the status quo by getting us to mistrust what we see through our own eyes—to deflect anger onto self-blame."[7]

Godfrey's first book, *Our Wildest Dreams: Women Making Money, Having Fun, Doing Good*[8] was the book that triggered her tenacious quest to find ways to help the next generation of girls and women acquire financial fluency as a tool for independence, confidence, safety, and daring. As Godfrey's work evolved, her writing documented her learning: *No More Frogs to Kiss* and *Twenty $ecrets to Money and Independence*[9] were published when she was still focused squarely on financial education for girls. As she realized that gender neutral financial education was another strategy for reaching girls, her writing became more inclusive. *Raising Financially Fit Kids*[10] was first published in 2003 and was recently revised and updated in 2013.

Today, Independent Means Inc. offers financial education for families—as well as exciting specialty programming designed for women, girls, families, and co-ed audiences.

The University of Maine Foundation honored Ms. Godfrey in June 2009 at the campus' seventy-fifth anniversary as one "who has gone on to serve their professions and their communities at the highest level:" "Joline D.

Godfrey of Santa Barbara, California, CEO of Independent Means, Inc., is an innovator in financial education for children and parents. Originator of a unique developmental approach to financial education, her work gives families new tools for raising children growing up in the midst of abundance."[11]

The Harvard Business School business case of Joline Godfrey and her "mentor" Jerry Sudbey, senior executive at Polaroid, tells the story of how the Photo Odyssee project (internal to Polaroid) became the entrepreneurial company "Odysseum." Case study readers are challenged to ask and answer the questions:

- Where does good mentoring end and meddling begin?
- How much support for intrapreneurship can you expect from a large corporate entity?
- How much of a mentor's credibility can be put on the line for a mentee's speculative ideas?
- When do you decide to stand on your own two feet or fly with your own wings?

Part B of the business case includes Godfrey's description of what she thinks a protégé is or ought to be:

"I like protégés who are learning junkies. I think that what keeps a mentor with you is the sense that they are getting stuff back, seeing things happen. This notion of someone taking care of you is a fallacy because a mentor who has to do all the work is going to run out of energy real soon. So your responsibility as a protégé is to feed them. [You] have a serious responsibility to give back. A good protégé understands what they owe and even if you don't give back directly to your mentor, you give back to someone, somewhere."[12]

Joline Godfrey is a wise woman who knows what it takes for us to establish financial literacy from the earliest possible years. She has transformed her message from one focused primarily on young girls into advice on how to create economic literacy throughout the life cycle—from the youngest family member (children as young as five) to retirees well into their later years. Her Community Development commentary at the Federal Reserve Bank of San Francisco in 1998 is worth reading and heeding over a decade later.

Lesson: ". . .[E]conomic education and development for adult women in our society is remedial. Economic education for girls on the other hand, is an investment, a sure-fire way to build economically strong communities."[13]

JILL KER CONWAY

Victoria first learned about Dr. Jill Ker Conway when a friend suggested she read her anthology, *Written by Herself: Autobiographies of American Women*, describing women who "overcame daunting obstacles to pursue their individual destinies in an often hostile, changing America."[14]

Later, Victoria discovered that Dr. Conway, herself, was just such an outstanding woman, born and raised on an outback tract of land called Coorain near Hillston, New South Wales, Australia, with her parents and her two brothers. Her early education was provided entirely by her mother and a governess. She graduated from the University of Sydney where she studied English and History. She received her PhD in history from Harvard and then taught history at the University of Toronto from 1964 to 1975. She also was vice president of internal affairs at the university from 1973 to 1975.[15]

Dr. Conway was professor of history and the first woman president of Smith College (Northampton, Massachusetts) from 1975 to 1985, where she introduced many innovations that helped young women advance financially and academically. She was a visiting scholar with the Massachusetts Institute of Technology's Program in Science, Technology and Society from 1985 through 2011.[16]

In 1978, she was named a director of Merrill Lynch, where she served on key board committees and finally as lead independent director until her retirement in April 2007. She was named a director of Colgate-Palmolive Company (1984–2010), served as a member of their audit committee, a member of their personnel and organization committee and chair of their nominating and corporate governance committee. She was a director of Nike Inc. (1987–2010), where she was a member of the nominating and corporate governance committee and chair of the corporate responsibility committee.[17] She came to that latter role after Nike experienced some of the earliest negative treatment for its overseas factory conditions and labor policies from about 1991 through 1999. Nike CEO Phil Knight initiated a top-down strategic re-direction that included the creation of the corporate responsibility committee at the board level. Jill Ker Conway chaired that committee after its inception in June 2001 until her retirement from the board in 2010.[18]

Dr. Conway served as a director of Lend Lease Corporation Limited for eleven years (beginning in 1992), became chairman of the board in November 2000, retiring in May 2003. Lend Lease Corporation Limited is an international real estate and financial services group.[19]

Dr. Conway has been a member of the Harvard University Board of Overseers and the Conference Board, a trustee of Hampshire College, Northfield Mt. Hermon School, the Clarke School for the Deaf, the Boston Museum Project, and the John F. Kennedy Library Foundation. Almost forty North American and Australian colleges, universities, and women's organizations have given Conway honorary degrees.

She has written or collaborated on more than twenty books including several about women in leadership and women's experiences in the eighteenth and nineteenth centuries. Her two volume anthology, *Written by Herself*,[20] represents some of the best biographical depictions of women's earliest professional and business successes. The story of her own life, *The Road from Coorain*,[21] based on her memoir by the same title, became an award-winning film in 2002.

On July 10, 2013, President Obama presented the 2012 National Humanities Medals (one of twelve awarded) to Jill Ker Conway, "author and leader in higher education, for her contributions as a historian and trailblazing academic leader." The award is bestowed by the National Endowment for the Humanities.[22] A month earlier (June 10, 2013), Conway received the Companion of the Order of Australia (AC) in the Queen's Birthday Honours List, Australia's highest civilian award.[23]

Dr. Conway continues to write and speak about women in leadership and in contemporary life.

Lesson: The journey to learn about the life and career of any woman begins with one story.

EVELYN Y. DAVIS

Happy birthday, Evelyn Yvonne DeJong Davis! Ms. Davis was 84 years old on August 16, 2013—born in Amsterdam, the Netherlands in 1929. She's called "Queen of the Corporate Jungle"[24] and "The Corporate Gadfly."[25] *People Magazine* called her "America's Most Dreaded Corporate Gadfly." *U.S. News & World Report* described her as "the woman they [chief executive officers] love to avoid."[26]

It is amazing that there is just one of her: one woman willing to challenge the corporate behemoths on their home turf, at their annual proxy meetings, which she's attended since 1960. Until her semi-retirement in 2012, it was said that she held about $700,000 in shares spread across 120 companies. She attended between 30 and 40 shareholder meetings annually.[27] For almost five decades, she produced an annual newsletter for corporate presidents and CEOs, *Highlights and Lowlights*, which she began publishing in

1963 to report on corporate governance, executive compensation, share-holder meetings, shareholder proposals, and selected regulatory actions.[28]

In 1989, she formed the Evelyn Y. Davis Foundation, through which she has donated generously to universities, business schools, arts organizations, museums and hospitals. In January 2004, she contributed $100,000 to the University of Pennsylvania to endow a scholarship for students pursuing careers in business or political journalism.[29] In May 2005, she gave $75,000 to support two National Trust Historic Sites, Cooper-Molera Adobe and Decatur House.[30] The gift also went to assist the renovation of the lobby at the National Trust's headquarters in Washington, D.C. In January 2007, another $100,000 gift went to the University of North Carolina at Chapel Hill's School of Journalism and Mass Communication to endow four annual scholarships for senior undergraduate students interested in careers in business journalism or political journalism.[31] In November 2007, $100,000 went to establish the Evelyn Y. Davis Fund at the Yale School of Management in support of the programs and activities of the Ira Millstein Center for Corporate Governance and Performance.[32] In January 2008, she gave $100,000 to support students in the University of Virginia's Darden Graduate School of Business Administration.[33] In 2008, she donated $100,000 to Riggs Emergency Department at Baylor University Medical Center at Dallas.[34] In December 2012, she donated $1 million to support the George Washington University School of Business and School of Medicine and Health Sciences[35] and a year later gave another $1 million to the National Press Foundation for the creation of a digital recording studios (to be called the Evelyn Davis Studios).[36]

On April Fools' Day, 2009, Ms. Davis rang the Closing Bell® for the New York Stock Exchange as it honored her contributions to the financial markets as an investor and shareholder advocate.[37] Did they pick that date or did she?

She's impressive, if abrasive. Sometimes we need that in our shareholders' meetings to make sure we're not being sold a bill of goods. She's earned the right to speak up and ask tough questions. She's bought the stock, has read the proxy statements, can distinguish good governance from bad, and knows when shareholders are being taken for a ride.

Lesson: Challengers have an obligation to make change happen, themselves.

GIRL TAXI

In the July 25, 2009, *Wall Street Journal* article, "'Girl Taxi' Service Offers Haven to Beirut's Women" by Don Duncan,[38] we learn that Nawal

Fashri, a business-minded Lebanese woman, invested successfully in a fleet of a dozen pink Peugeots tooling around Beirut twenty-four hours a day, providing safe and essential transportation to women, and earning $200,000 in sales this year. Brava to Banet Taxi ("girl taxi")! The business idea is also succeeding in Dubai, Tehran, and Cairo—all locations in which the Muslim faith bars women from driving and prohibits unchaperoned interactions between genders. The result is a new market: women having a great demand for secure taxi services offered by women.

Lesson: Not only is invention the mother of necessity, but it also seems as if mother is an inventor of necessity.

V. S. SHIRLEY

The 1979 second gas crisis in the United States (like the 1973 predecessor) resulted in a push favoring carpooling, mass transit, and enhanced use of technology to eliminate the commute to work, itself. Advocates called the latter, "telecommuting," although the original concept was "telework"—an idea brought to life to serve totally different purposes by a British businesswoman, V. S. Shirley, in 1962.

Kelly was a consultant to area cities, counties, and the state's department of transportation in how to develop telework programs. In that role, Kelly tapped the wisdom and lessons provided by Mrs. Shirley, who established a globally recognized company, ascended to corporate board roles, and provided insight into the challenges and opportunities that a technology career offered to women.

"May women soon cease to think of themselves as a minority," Dame Stephanie Shirley emailed Kelly when she wrote asking about the early foundations of telecommuting. Mrs. Shirley's message was to seek out women who thought, as she did, as if they already had equal access to equal opportunity. "You achieve the goal you aim at: if you aim at failure, you will succeed."

Vera Stephanie Shirley created the business concept of telework. She formed and operated a software and application development business at a company she called F International (F as in "Freelance"), which was dedicated to providing opportunities for people to work at home. The mission of her firm was:

to stay a leader in the rapidly growing and highly profitable knowledge intensive software industry. . . to achieve this by developing, through modern telecommunications, the unutilized intellectual energy of individuals and groups unable to work in a conventional environment.[39]

V. S. ("Steve") Shirley was born September 16, 1933, in Dortmund, Germany. She came with her sister, Renate, to England in 1939 from Vienna, Austria, as an unaccompanied child refugee from the Nazi Holocaust on a "Kindertransport" operated by the Quakers.[40]

She took evening classes and received a degree (with honors) from London University in 1956. She married Derek George Millington Shirley in 1959, and they had one son, Giles, born in 1963. Giles was found to be profoundly mentally handicapped and, at 13 years of age, was put in the care of a home associated with a local mental hospital. He was diagnosed as autistic in 1968, which led to Mrs. Shirley's extensive involvement in charitable efforts on behalf of autistic individuals and their families. She founded The Kingwood Trust charity (1993) to provide long-term care for adults with profound learning difficulties. Giles died in 1998.

Beginning in 1959, Steve Shirley worked as a highly-skilled software developer and junior manager for the computer consulting entity Computer Developments Ltd. (CDL), a subsidiary of ICL.[41] She left the firm in 1962, planning to have her first child and realizing that a professional corporate career was incompatible with her goal of putting family priorities in the balance. She started her own business, Freelance Programmers Ltd. in 1962, working on the dining room table in her home. By 1964, there were a dozen other self-employed people working on a contract basis out of their homes.

Freelance Programmers Ltd. became F International, employing 100 people by 1970. In 1985, when it became F.I Group PLC, it employed over 1,000 people and had revenues of U.S. $10 million a year. By then, it was the twentieth largest computer consultancy and software house in Britain, with offices in London, Holland and Denmark.

In 1978, Mrs. Shirley established an American branch as a subsidiary of another firm in Tarrytown, New York, and Oakland, California. They found the American working women of that era had more degrees; were more interested in sales than in project management; and generally, were not interested in part-time contract work at home. That joint arrangement was discontinued in 1984.

In 1985, F International collaborated with the Bristol Department of Transportation in one of the earliest of "intelligent vehicle highway systems" (or "roadway telematics," to use the British expression). F International designed, and the city built, a computerized highway accident prevention system that provided feedback from sensors built into the road in a dangerous fog-bound area.

Two types of workers were employed at F International. The first type was "panel workers:" the firm's freelance workers who contracted to work for the company on a project by project basis. The other type was "salaried workers:" primarily those in management, sales and clerical support areas.

Of the firm's total staff of 1,078 people in 1985, 817 were panel workers (all of whom were employed part time), while 261 were salaried workers (half part time, half full time). Of the panel workers, 96 percent were women; 90 percent of them had young children. Panel workers received few employment benefits. They averaged 20–30 hours per week and 26–40 weeks per year. The heavy reliance on panel or contract workers meant that F International could keep fixed costs down and respond flexibly to business fluctuations. F International invested heavily in project control and communications, which, according to Mrs. Shirley, were a main reason for F International's success. Over time, the business concept of moving labor from a fixed cost to a variable cost category led to the corporation's outsourcing all but the core of their business activities.

Later in the evolution of the firm, Mrs. Shirley pointed to the establishment of neighborhood local centers as another response to panelist concerns. Work centers were located so as to maximize staff catchment areas, as alternatives to sales offices in the city's center. These neighborhood work centers also promoted teamwork and shared use of networks.

Mrs. Shirley faced unique challenges as a female technical professional in the 1960s and 1970s. She went by the name of Steve Shirley, using the shortened form of her middle name, Stephanie, so as to overcome "uncertainties" that might arise in businessmen's minds about contracting with a female entrepreneur. Sales letters signed as if from a man got a better response, according to Mrs. Shirley.

In an interview with her, the following exchange revealed her awareness of contemporary business realities:

Q. Have you found that when you market your services to clients, they have difficulty accepting this organization, this form of working?

A: The main problem is that they don't see how project management works. There's no doubt that we have difficulty in opening new accounts. That's why we're very conscious of our image. For instance, if you interview any of our staff, we wouldn't allow you to take a photo of a woman at home with a baby. . . . Clients are not going to entrust their precious stock control to a company that looks like a nursery.[42]

Another aspect of F International's success was support and encouragement from the British government. The firm was able to keep at home, in England, those skilled programmers who otherwise might never be used or who might have been part of the British brain drain to other international competitors. Further, F International was capable of employing physically challenged individuals who benefited from the company's opportunities for flexible work and lifestyle.

F International and its several subsidiary companies became F.I. Group PLC in 1985. F.I. Group began a workforce stock buy-in program in 1991 which reached 49 percent of the employees owning corporate stock by 1994. Stock was sold to both "associates" (the new term for panel workers) and full-time employees alike. In 1994, the conglomerate consisted of FI Systems (providing the core business support and maintenance programming), FI Partners (the firm that formed "strategic alliances in IT outsourcing," as for example when it adopted the systems staff of Whitbread PLC and the Cooperative Bank PLC), F.I. Scotland (the regional offices of the North Country), FI Kernel (the client-server technology center), FI Training, and FI Recruitment Ltd.

Mrs. Shirley retired from FI Group as "honorary Life President" in 1993, at which time the firm reported turnover of $75 million and a total enterprise headcount of 1,600 persons, with systems and training work orders running to the millennium.

In March 1996, F.I. Group stock was floated on the London Stock Exchange. In April 2001, the company changed its name to Xansa. Beginning in July 2007, Xansa PLC started to be taken private through a buy-out by Groupe Steria SCA, which was completed with the London Stock Exchange delisting of Xansa in October 2007. In March 2008, the merged entity was rebranded as Steria.[43]

Mrs. Shirley became a fellow of the British Computer Society (1970) and its president between 1989 and 1990. She was a consulting editor to John Wiley & Sons Publishing in the information processing field from 1978 through 1987. She served as a member of several professional certification boards, including the Computer Systems and Electronics Requirements Board (1979–1981), the Electronics and Avionics Requirements Board (1981–1983), the Council of the Industrial Society (1984–1990); and the Open Tech (1983–1986), which developed the concept of distance learning.

She became a companion of the British Institute of Management (1984), a freeman of the City of London (1987) and a vice president of the City and Guilds of London Institute (2000–2005). She was a founding

Assistant to the Court of The Worshipful Company of Information Technologists, and become one of the few women to have headed a "livery company" (in the City of London, a guild focused on charitable and educational activities).

Mrs. Shirley was invested as Dame Commander, Order of the British Empire (OBE, 1990) for her services to the information technology industry. She received the Recognition of Information Technology Achievement Award (1985), the British Institute of Management Gold Medal (1991), and several honorary fellowships and degrees. In 1995, she was honored by the U.S. National Women's Hall of Fame.

In 2003, she was awarded the Beacon Fellowship Prize for startups in recognition of her years of dedication to and financial support of innovative charities serving autism and information technology.

Mrs. Shirley was the first commercial director (1992–2000) to AEA Technology PLC, a company which grew out of the UK Atomic Energy Authority. She became the first non-American director on the board of Tandem Computers Inc. (1992-1997).[44]

She established the Shirley Foundation in 1996 through which she has donated over $100 million for programs supporting autism research and advocacy and for innovations in information technology. In 1998, the Shirley Foundation established Prior's Court School as an exceptional school for children with autism. The first pupils arrived in September 1999, and the school was officially opened by the Princess Royal in May 2000.

Through support of the Shirley Foundation, the Oxford Internet Institute in May 2001 became the world's first truly multidisciplinary entity based at a major university and focused on the social, ethical, and other issues raised by the Internet.[45] In 2004, Mrs. Shirley joined the board of directors of the U.S. National Alliance for Autism Research and established its equivalent in the UK (later rebranded as Autistica).

Mrs. Shirley was one of the first to concentrate on the social and economic aspects of the computing business, including the transfer of work into the home, distance learning, and the use of computing as a communication aid for people with disabilities. She pioneered workforce participation and, starting in the 1970s, gradually transferred control of FI to its workforce including the associates.

In 2012, she published her memoirs in a book titled *Let IT Go: The Story of the Entrepreneur Turned Ardent Philanthropist*[46] and continues speaking, writing, and working in philanthropic endeavors that support innovative autism research and information technology applications.

If we look only at the challenges defining her life, we might have focused on a youth of the Holocaust, a child in a strange land without her parents, a woman in a man's world struggling in technology at its most formative stage, the mother of a child with learning disabilities later diagnosed as autism, and a parent who lost a child. By those criteria alone, we might have missed Dame Shirley's seven-plus decades of innovative workforce management; her creation of telecommuting, telework and neighborhood centers concepts; her multi-million dollar business ultimately transferred to the control and the benefit of the employees; her unprecedented honors on multiple continents; and her unparalleled investment in charitable ventures serving families facing autism and a society struggling with the consequences of highly wired global networks.

Lesson: Women in leadership demonstrate something truly unique if we would be willing to learn from their successes as much as from their challenges.

SHEILA RONNING

When asked to reveal her secret to networking, Sheila Ronning said, "Be fearless, sincere, honest, and frank. Always be the real you—the authentic you."

Sheila Ronning learned her networking and alliance-building collaborative skills as an active member of business-oriented associations in the greater Minneapolis/St. Paul, Minnesota, area. She was a member of several chapters of the Chambers of Commerce (Minneapolis Regional, St. Paul, Edina, Metro North, and TwinWest) and of the Minnesota Chapter of the National Association of Women Business Owners (NAWBO). She was named a board member to several of these organizations. She served on the Strategic Marketing Committee for WomenVenture, the Business Advisory Group for Lifeworks Services, and the Small Business Committee for the Minneapolis Chamber.

In April 1996, after eight years in operations, sales, and merchandising management at Best Buys, Sheila chartered her own ship and realized her passion for marketing, public relations, networking, event coordination, and strategy by forming SHARP UpSwing, a marketing and events management firm based in Edina, Minnesota. Her event planning strategy integrated just the right mix of services for budget-conscious leaders at some of the area's largest business associations.

As a Minnesota NAWBO member, Sheila built a reputation for her ability to "bring people into the room" at NAWBO events. Dee

Thibodeau, CEO of Charter Solutions and a member of the board at NAWBO, saw great potential in this young, enthusiastic entrepreneur and asked her if she would consider organizing and marketing events for the Minnesota chapter. Sheila respected and admired Dee and accepted the assignment for SHARP UpSwing to sell corporate sponsorships, figure out how to fundraise, secure corporate members, and grow the organization's membership.

Sheila describes their relationship as "an informal mentorship—I'd go to her for advice. I respected her insight. More importantly, I listened to her suggestions and followed through."

Sheila created the UpSwing Business EXPO in 1997 after gathering feedback from her clients about how difficult it was for them to build business connections. The EXPO grew into the largest business-to-business networking event in the Twin Cities.

After a few years of seeing me easily fill a room at the EXPO and NAWBO events, Dee approached me with an idea. She said "I would love it if you would start an event that focused on helping women serve on corporate boards." This wasn't an area I was familiar with, but Dee is a smart, savvy business woman whom I respect so I figured she was onto something! In November 2002, I had my 1st annual event in Minneapolis which became Women in the Boardroom. The event provided information to women about why serve on a corporate board, what happens in the board room, and how to get yourself qualified to serve.

After a few years of capacity attendance at the Minneapolis Women in the Boardroom events, Dee once again approached Sheila and said, "You need to take this to other women in other cities and states." Chicago was the first city added in 2006. In the next four years, Women in the Boardroom events were held in 15 cities across the nation.

"I am only one of the many fortunate women that Dee chooses to help guide and mentor. She is someone that many women look up to. Whatever Dee tells you, if you are smart, you will take it and run with it," said Sheila.

Dee Thibodeau's perspective is this:

Sheila is modest—it was a tough beginning for her. No matter what situation she found herself in, she forged ahead. It didn't matter what trials or tribulations she encountered. Like any real entrepreneur, Sheila discovered that business goes up and down, but you have to move ahead—no matter what. The reality is that Sheila has surpassed any ideas I've ever had of expanding Women in the Boardroom. Every year and everywhere, she keeps moving women forward.

The Minneapolis/St. Paul Business Journal honored Sheila as one of the top 25 "Women to Watch" in the Twin Cities in 2002. Other local accolades continued to highlight the success of the Women in the Boardroom panels, where women executives and sitting directors told women, in no uncertain terms, what they needed to do to take their careers to the next level. Sheila was honored by the TwinWest Chamber of Commerce as an "Entrepreneur of the Year" finalist in 2005 for her positive impact on the small business community. She won the "Changemaker Award" from Minnesota NAWBO in 2005. Sheila was featured in Dick Youngblood's column in the *Star Tribune* in 2005.[47] The Minneapolis/St. Paul Business Journal named Sheila to their prestigious "40 Under Forty" list in 2006 for her entrepreneurial dynamism and reputation as a networking maven.

The recognitions continued. Sheila was a winner of the 2010 Enterprising Women of the Year Award from Enterprising Woman's Magazine and named a 2010 "Minnesotan on the Move" by Finance & Commerce. Sheila's leadership development expertise was featured in the *Wall Street Journal*, *ForbesWoman*, the *Chicago Sun-Times*, the *Star Tribune*, the *Pioneer Press*, *Upsize Minnesota*, and *dbaWomen on Networking*.

Sheila now had taken her own first steps toward working with an advisory board of local women executives and leaders in Minnesota, including Dee Thibodeau. At the start, it consisted of an "annual check in"—a business update over lunch. Dee described the evolution of Sheila's board: "Women gave different viewpoints, and then Sheila decided which direction to take."

The national events began to pull Sheila in multiple directions as women in each city wanted more opportunities to learn about women in leadership and women on boards. The topic was reaching headline levels not only nationally, but internationally.

Sheila kept hearing recommendations that she establish a hub in New York, which would put her at the center of more women executives per square mile than any other city in the country. Sheila had always wanted to live and work in New York. It was a tough choice: all of her family and network had been well established in the Twin Cities area, yet so much of the business potential was in the Greater New York area. Sheila was torn between sailing out on her own to unknown waters or holding on to the familiar and safe harbor that had taken her to this point.

Sheila moved to New York City in May of 2011, knowing only one woman there and leaving her network back in Minneapolis. Up to this point, the Great Recession had not hit Women in the Boardroom; but, just a few months after moving her life and business to a new city, things took a turn for the worse.

We started losing sponsorship dollars left and right, and if that wasn't enough, women stopped attending events because they had to be nose down at work. I had to make some tough choices: either give up what I had worked so hard to accomplish and go back to work for someone else or immediately turn this ship in a new direction. But I didn't even know what direction! Not only was I not sure what to do professionally, but I kept thinking that I'd have to leave New York and go back to being the person I used to be. Moving to New York from the Midwest was intimidating, but I loved the challenge of being somewhere new. I decided my first step was to get back to doing what I do best—to network! I networked my butt off in New York. I kept meeting one amazing woman after another—all of whom wanted to help me figure out the new direction for Women in the Boardroom.

I also realized that I had to lose this "intimidation" I was feeling about New York City. I needed to find me in this new setting. It was such a relief to start sharing my story with these women. They simply embraced me. They helped me figure out how to turn the ship.

Just like her clients, Sheila had to re-assess her business strategy. "My vision has always been to do things that really count and make a difference in people's lives." So, Sheila tapped the wisdom of her personal relationships, opened up new dialogs with her advisors, and accepted the challenge of "the new normal" head on.

She stayed in touch with a woman in Boston, "Susan Hammond, an advisor to top level corporations, [who] suggested I put together a cross-nation executive or advisory council to help me with this new transition in my business." Sheila started holding conference calls with the group, then evolved it into a one-on-one relationship to tap their insight on specific subjects.

Dee Thibodeau was always there for me, but I never want to be a drain on one mentor. I've been fortunate to be able to surround myself with really amazing, smart women. And I reached out to them all.

Once I began to open up and ask for help from the women, they responded enthusiastically. "We've got to do whatever we can to help you," they told me. Women like Alice Krause of NewsonWomen.com rallied around me with ideas to help make Women in the Boardroom work.

Carol Morley (who had been a panelist on the topic of "Critical Thinking: Cultivating a Mindset of Success," told me to stop traveling and focus instead on growing our impact in the local market.

Changes were underway. Sheila decided in August/September 2011 to cut back on nationwide events, substituting webinars, the LinkedIn group Women in the Boardroom, and a more focused membership strategy to deliver high value content to serious women board candidates.

More advice came her way.

Don't focus on the mass market, but rather on senior women who were qualified and interested in board roles and, thus, the board expertise Women in the Boardroom has to offer. Roll out a membership strategy of tiered levels with a premium membership level.

I was open to all of these new ideas—I took myself out of the way of growing the business. I brought in other experts like Debra Nelms to handle the board coaching. I brought in Cortney Mohnk as project manager to manage membership coordination. I let people help me succeed.

Our numbers tell the Women in the Boardroom performance story. In just the first six months of 2011, we had a total of 165 premium members of which ten were top tier VIP members. By 2013, we'd grown to 199 premium members of which ninety-eight were at the VIP level.

After an initial rollout in 2012, we now have nine corporate members. Our LinkedIn group currently has over 5,600 members. We have 7,600 followers on Twitter and just opened a Facebook page which now has 600 followers.

We just started marketing the idea that Women in the Boardroom had qualified board-eligible women. In the first year we received twenty-nine notifications about board opportunities from across the country. This past year, we sent out communications about fifty board-ready candidates which resulted in twenty board interviews.

Just like the story of the evolution of Women in the Boardroom, there is no one perfect way to get onto a board. We are making the kind of progress that we envisioned. And, along the way, we are showing women how to "show up, stand up, and speak up." That's no small achievement.

Dee Thibodeau sees the long term success on the horizon.

When Sheila decided to focus on very qualified women, companies took note of her business, and boards of directors realized the unique value and expertise her company provided them. When boards have "moved the needle" by adding more women directors, Sheila's name will be there as the "Fiery Woman Who Made It Happen!"

Sheila Ronning currently is an in-demand speaker on the topics of "Personal Authenticity" and "Voice, Vision, Presence." In describing her experience transitioning from Minnesota to New York and through the Great Recession, Sheila likes to quote the Japanese author Haruki Murakami.

Lesson: "And once the storm is over you won't remember how you made it through, how you managed to survive. You won't even be sure, in fact, whether the storm is really over. But one thing is certain. When you come out of the storm you won't be the same person who walked in. That's what this storm's all about."[48]

FIVE

In the Media: Mentorship Stories in Published Works or about the Media Itself

There comes a time when mentors are more consciously chosen. We choose how we would be influenced and by whom. As the Transcendental Society saying goes, "When the student is ready to learn, the master will appear." We choose our role models and our sources of influence as much, if not more, than they choose us.

Much of what is presented as "reality" about women in leadership comes to us from a wide variety of media messages. The stories told in magazines, especially, but also in books, journals, newspapers, and other publications may not always tell us what we are or are becoming but, rather, may focus exclusively on where we have been. Our capacity to know the difference between myth and reality defines our judgment.

Reading books based on quality interviews and research provides mentorship if one is willing to learn to "think differently" through the experience of having one's presumptions challenged. Those challenges can include acknowledging and celebrating the achievements of other women. It can also allow recognition of one's own ambition in a chosen field of interest. The advice of authors who have thought long and hard about networking, under-earning, and financial self-sufficiency provides mentorship that might not be available from family, school, peers, or work.

Movies, as much as magazines, have conditioned women to think about themselves (to socialize themselves) in predictable and small-minded perspectives. As more women take the initiative and enter media industries, there will be a greater likelihood that we will be able to alter those media-formed self-perceptions. That, in and of itself, is mentoring.

As we speak, so we will be heard. Mentors today are coaching women to pitch themselves and their business ideas more effectively. Great mentors tell us how we can improve ourselves for our own satisfaction, not merely to please others.

Mentors who are advocating the importance of science, technology, engineering, and math (STEM) education and careers offer special insight into the learning, growth, and satisfaction that can be tapped.

The publication industry offers opportunities to educate and mentor women in diverse fields. If we want to alter the self-image of women aspiring to leadership, we probably will need to see more women willing to take the reins as the head of more publishing entities.

IN THE COMPANY OF WOMEN

One of the most insightful books about how women view other women is *In the Company of Women*,[1] written by Pat Heim, PhD, and Susan A. Murphy, PhD, MBA. It is a powerful book that should be read in its entirety. This summary just touches the surface of its message. If women would mentor other women successfully, then they must understand the dynamics presented in this book. Their message is eye-opening, if not scary. Even more important is to observe how the book reveals its essential truth ITRW ("in the real world").

Before her ouster as head of Hewlett-Packard, Carly Fiorina was considered one of the most powerful women in public corporate life (by most men). She used to say that "gender didn't matter"[2] in her climb to the top rungs of the corporate ladder. Then, in her first speech after the fall, she talked instead about how the boys at AT&T dubbed her a "token bimbo" and described other prejudices from her rising-star competitive peers at Hewlett-Packard who tried to "diminish and disgrace" her.[3]

The female reaction to Carly's post-HP commencement speech at North Carolina Agricultural and Technical State University (NC A&T) was softer, more accepting, and more tolerant than was their response to her earlier speech in May 2004 at Simmons College (Boston), where she had been more assertive:

Women are more comfortable with a powerful woman [like Carly post-HP] who plays down her importance rather than one who does not.[4]

There it was, in all its glory: the "Power Dead-Even Rule." Even Carly Fiorina had to, finally, re-balance the Power–Relationships–Self-Esteem triangle to enable women to feel more comfortable with her, more accepting of her as a "powerful woman," by playing down her importance and by sharing "trouble talk." It was as if Carly had the book hidden under her robe.

Heim and Murphy describe the phenomenon of "female–to–female conflict" as indirect or covert aggression.[5] Women attack women they perceive to be more powerful in such a way as to remain hidden, undetected, in order to avoid retaliation or social condemnation. Women are "catty."

Whew! What a scary concept! Think "ambush" and consider the synonyms women use to describe the phenomenon: gossip, divulging secrets, spreading rumors, publicly making insinuating or insulting comments, undermining, sabotaging, or purposefully snubbing or withdrawing friendship.

Heim and Murphy explained why this occurs. They discovered that women were struggling to maintain a balance among the three forces:

Power–Relationships–Self-esteem

Power is the external influence one wields in the outside world. **Self-esteem** is the internal power one feels: the sense of inner strength and self-worth. **Relationships** are connections to other people.[6]

Heim and Murphy describe **relationships** as the keystone for women. "The importance of social interactions in the workplace is the most significant difference between the genders,"[7] they said, contrasting women's relationships with men's hierarchies.

Women think and work along relational lines. Women's collaborative leadership style is dramatically different from men's: the former share information and involve others in the decision-making process. Heim and Murphy observed that "females do not use conflicts to establish a hierarchy; [instead,] their quarrels revolve around access to resources."[8]

Hierarchies are structures for re-enforcing men's beliefs about themselves and their self-esteem. Hierarchies result from competition: the creation of social structures that are predictable and orderly and that prevent anarchy among males.[9] Hierarchies do *not* serve the same needs for women. They do not prevent "anarchy" among women. In fact, the existence of hierarchies may create an environment that fosters "anarchy" or a sense of imbalance (unevenness) among women.[10]

Today, inclusion and diversity networks abound inside corporations in an attempt to attract and retain women in the workplace. These are attempts to foster relationships among women in a male-dominated corporation. Women may not enjoy or appreciate the climb up the hierarchical ladder as their male counterparts do, resulting in women suffering from a sense of loss of relationships in the work environment. Women find little in the sterile workplace environment that might contribute to their sense of personal achievement.

Heim and Murphy describe **power** as simply "the ability to get things done."[11] Power does not exist in a vacuum or in isolation from the individual. Men consider power an end in and of itself, while women consider power more as a means to achieving other goals.

The authors described several types of power: reward power, coercive power, legitimate power, expert power, referent power, and associative power.[12] More importantly, for women, unlike men, "power flows through their relationships, not from external symbols."[13]

Women have the "Chip Theory of Power," somewhat similar to the male concept of "Markers."[14] Women strive toward equity (evenness), while men strive toward inequality (unevenness) or personal, competitive advantage. Women try to keep the chips even, while men strive to increase their individual share of the markers. If the chips are uneven, women expect a re-balancing in order to be comfortable.

Thus, women felt uncomfortable with the earlier Carly when she appeared to have all that power. Later, when Carly downplayed her power by talking about how she, too, felt discrimination, women felt more at ease with her. The power chips were re-balanced.

Self-esteem is the final part of the balancing act—one's sense of worth in one's own eyes, according to Heim and Murphy. Self-esteem is the power that one allows oneself to have. It is the ability to form an identity and attach a value to it.

Heim and Murphy cite many examples of research showing that, normally, there is a correlation between high self-esteem and high achievement (which can lead to the accrual of power). However, for many women, "all the perceived power in the world won't build their self-esteem—they view themselves as unworthy."[15]

- The imposter syndrome: a self-defeating attitude, a feeling that you will be "found out" as unworthy
- A feeling of lack of competence, skill, or intelligence (contrary to objective data)
- A sense that one doesn't deserve the success and the perks
- A fear of one's inability to repeat past successes; a conviction that previous accomplishments were a fluke
- A belief that success has not come from one's own efforts or abilities, but rather from fate, luck, timing, charm, or manipulation[16]

". . . [W]hen [women] experience interpersonal discord, they often disparage themselves as inadequate, which cuts into their positive sense of self."[17]

When women perceive their self-esteem is low, the triangle is out of kilter. Women may not be able to change their internal sense of self, to re-establish balance of the triangle, so an alternative strategy is to bring other women of power down to their level. Thus, we see the full array of "sabotage savvy" behavior on the part of uncertain women.[18]

This is Heim and Murphy's core concept of the "Power Dead-Even Rule" at play: "an invisible natural law that operates behind the scenes, shapes our relations to other women in our lives, explains the connection among relationships, power and self-esteem."[19]

When their sense of power *or* sense of relationships *or* self-esteem are not enhanced in the interaction with others, women tend to re-balance the triangle through destructive behaviors intended to bring others down to their perceived, lower level. At that point, women are "in the company of women": demonstrating indirect aggression and hurting each other and themselves.

Lesson: The "Power Dead-Even Rule" explains significant portions of women's behavior toward other women, including mentorship relationships.

DIAGNOSIS AND TREATMENT

What do you do if you sense, in yourself, that out-of-kilter feeling that leads to an attack on another woman in leadership? If that internal imbalance prevents you from mentoring another or from being mentored, then you will not be able to tap the wisdom that surrounds you. Instead, you will remain stuck.

The first task is to recognize the source of the imbalance: the "Power Dead-Even Rule" described by Pat Heim and Susan Murphy in their book *In the Company of Women*. One leg of the personal trilogy of power, relationship, or self-esteem must be inadequate to uphold the entire person. First comes the diagnosis, and then the treatment can follow.

Which one of the senses is causing the limp? In the company of this particular woman, as you compare yourself with her in your own mind, you feel powerless, lacking a basis for a relationship, or your self-esteem is challenged. What are you sensing and why? Even before this assessment can be made, we must first acknowledge the reality that it is unlikely that this woman did anything to cause the out-of-sync sensation you are experiencing—it is entirely in your own head, in your own perception of yourself relative to her.

Once you can recognize that it is you who feels less powerful, or that it is you who has an inadequate store of relationships, or that you have low self-esteem, then you realize that those feelings arise when you view, listen to, or encounter this particular woman. Seeing a woman of achievement triggers these sensations in you. She does not "make you feel this way." She is a mirror of your feelings: you are seeing yourself (or rather your own perceived shortcomings) in her reflection. You did not acknowledge these sensations in yourself until you saw something in her as a mirror.

The diagnosis has to examine what hurts about your comparison of yourself with this person you believe to be whole or healthy, unlike yourself. It is easy to paint all of your feelings the deep green of envy and jealousy: she's richer, has a better husband, more toys or things, more beautiful children, a better job, bigger bonuses, a nicer wardrobe, more awards, more degrees, more promotions, or whatever. That personal check list must be turned on its head: you need to see it as your personal list of things you don't have or didn't do. Then you need to look at that list and ask yourself, truly and deeply, are you sure those are the things that you really want or need?

Too often, women will look at another woman and only see "the grass looks greener" over there, without any true assessment of what it takes to maintain that appearance or even whether that is something that the woman considers important in her life. Mentoring among women often becomes a situation where one woman wants what the other woman appears to have achieved. "I wish I had what she had. If only she would mentor me, I'd learn what she learned. I'd have what she has."

Mentoring expectations among women often are based on weakness and sacrifice. The woman at the bottom wants help to become something she has not become, while the woman at the top wants help to have the relationships that she feels she's missing at the top. Both are running on empty. Mentoring on these foundations ends up not being worth the effort for either.

One way to rebalance the triangle is to affirm the most admirable trait that you perceive in the women with whom you are comparing yourself. If the "Power Dead-Even Rule" says that women tend to bring down others whom they envy, then another way to obey that rule is to pull up that part of yourself that you perceive to be short by comparison. This is "tapping the wisdom that surrounds you"—replenishing the empty well.

For example, when you see an elite runner on a training run, you have a choice of criticizing her form in a fit of jealous pique or of admiring features of her form that you might incorporate into your style to enhance your own stride or pace. It is your choice. The former will leave you with nothing but the empty feeling of hating someone who does it better than you do. The latter provides you with insight into what you might do to enhance your own performance.

Other examples come closer to home. Many women have great difficulty, even in their mature years, acknowledging the contributions of their own mothers. This may be where the "Power Dead-Even Rule" gets its start. Many women carry these envious feelings into the workplace: having trouble acknowledging the contributions of more senior women or women who lead them. Others have problems acknowledging the success of women political leaders—holding them to impossibly high standards that no human being could satisfy.

The "Power Dead-Even Rule" is all about re-establishing one's own personal sense of emotional equilibrium when confronted by perceived differences. If women have not yet learned how to keep their balance in the dialog with other women of achievement, they may find that they have similar problems when they encounter men whom they perceive to be stronger, more successful, or more assertive. Learning from outstanding women provides a safe and comfortable means of building one's self-esteem and confidence to encounter any meaningful engagement.

Lesson: You can pull yourself upward in comparison to others as easily as you can pull them down in your esteem. "Tapping the wisdom that surrounds you" ensures that you and the person with whom you are comparing yourself have the opportunity to rise to your greatest potentials.

NECESSARY DREAMS

Anna Fels's book *Necessary Dreams*,[20] provides perspective and light around ambition: that very blurry picture woman have trouble putting into focus.

Dr. Fels is a practicing psychiatrist in New York City who has written for *The New York Times Book Review*, the *Times Literary Supplement, The Nation, Self*, and, most recently, the "Science Times" section of *The New York Times*. She is a member of the faculty of the Weill Medical College of Cornell University at New York Presbyterian Hospital and has written a Harvard Business Review article entitled, "Do Women Lack Ambition?"[21]

Her work focuses on the question of why women feel anxiety or are evasive about having ambition. Why do women hesitate to admit they aspire to anything: power, position, influence, money, wealth, achievement, or success? Why do women bang back the nail that tries to stick out—those women who do strive to be different and to succeed? Why do women *not* cheer each other on, slap each other on the back, encourage each other along their chosen paths?

Reviewers say that Fels "examines the mixed messages that women get about claiming recognition."[22] In her own words, Fels says:

> *Throughout their lives women are subtly discouraged from pursuing goals by a pervasive lack of recognition for their accomplishments. Parents, peers, teachers, professors, bosses and institutions all underrate work by females and therefore unwittingly withhold appropriate praise and support. All too often girls and young women incrementally lose their early convictions about their abilities and talents. A belief in the likelihood of achieving their goals slowly fades and is supplanted by aspiration for more socially available types of attention; particularly attention for sexual attractiveness.[23]*

How could this possibly be true? Anna Fels's research resonates. She suggests that women search for the affirmation and recognition of their contributions just about as much as men do. Yet, they tend not to get either affirmation or recognition. Instead, they're more likely to get labeled "feminist," "liberal," "not a nice girl," or worse.

Does this describe what women have been trying to tell us as they "opt out" of corporate America? Were they too nice to tell us the truth—that working inside the halls and gatherings of corporate top rungs was an unrewarding, unsatisfying, lonesome, frustrating, and discouraging experience? Did they conclude that changing a filthy diaper gave greater satisfaction? Whew!

Does this describe what women are experiencing when they tell us in surveys that they felt left out of the key meetings and conversations of the top corporate world? They felt excluded from real acknowledgement of their contributions. They felt used or undervalued.

Fels suggests that women search for affirmation and recognition of their contributions just as much as men do, yet women tend not to get the positive feedback. Not from supervisors. Not from peers. Not from spouses. Not even from their emotional sisters. In fact, most of these sources of potential "atta girls" end up delivering what Fels calls "a mixed message"—how gentle of her. It's a message that says "don't outshine your boss," "don't upstage your husband," and "don't make your peers look bad." If a woman dares to aspire, she can expect to feel the subtle intimidation of innuendo that suggests she's probably not good in bed, not a good mother or wife, or otherwise just another "uppity broad."

There is a tendency to believe that this problem is only true for those who went through the 1960s and 1970s feminist era. We assume that this isn't a problem faced by today's women. Of course, today, women are getting their due recognition, equal opportunity, and encouragement toward advancement. Sure. Right.

If these problems describe the world that women experience in the workplace as they attempt to rise to leadership roles, how could they possibly be expected to mentor other up-and-coming women? If they do not find satisfaction and affirmation themselves, why would they encourage others to follow in their footsteps?

Dr. Fels, as a psychiatrist, offers some possible "treatments" for this disease:

- Think carefully about your goals and your future
- know the enemy (cultural bias, a bad employer, a conniving friend or peer)
- Get on the same page with your mate for balancing work–family life
- Lobby Congress to pass more family-friendly laws
- Seek out mentors
- Seek out peers who acknowledge your accomplishments

The first three recommendations are sound. First, dream your dream, whatever it may be, and plan your future as if you own it, because you do. Second, trust your intuition when you confront those who would undervalue you for their own reasons—be wary, be aware, and be not caught up in their assessment of you or your goals and dreams. The third is crucial—your mate can provide the good counsel, encouragement, and the solace you may not find anywhere else. But it is a negotiated settlement that must constantly be re-negotiated over time.

The ephemeral faith in legislative solutions is a source of many false hopes. Women are all too familiar with the reality that laws that were passed in one environment can too easily be repealed in another. And even after passage of a law, there is an even longer row to hoe to enforce the laws. When women recognize the power they possess in the electoral process and actually elect a significantly greater share of sympathetic legislators into positions of power, this option will become a source of change.

Seeking out mentors also is worthy, but a strategy facing challenges. The important question to be addressed is, "What is there in you that warrants being mentored? Coached? Developed?"

It's more than simply giving out trophies for effort. Ambitious women are those who stay in the game and demonstrate leadership. And, once there, they have the choice of encouraging other women also to aspire and of recognizing the women who helped them get there.

Finding peers who give women the acknowledgement and recognition they deserve is the essence of team- and alliance-building, which are two critical career skills women can and must learn. Asking for help, letting go of control, delegating, and taking the chance that someone might not perform as well or might take the limelight. All of these are components of working with others. Risky business. No guarantees.

All of these are viable alternatives. In addition, women must live by the rule "to thine own self be true." Give yourself as much acknowledgement, recognition, and celebration as you can possibly stand. As a woman, you will have a gigantic inner void that needs to be filled, so start filling it up yourself. And keep doing it.

Two, "give better than you get." Give those other women who deserve recognition and admiration all that you can spare. Celebrate the accomplishments and achievements of the women you know and admire. They, too, will have a gigantic inner void that needs to be filled, so start helping them fill it up as well. And keep doing it.

The third comes from a phrase in the poem *Desiderata:*[24]

You are a child of the universe
no less than the trees and the stars;
you have a right to be here.

Lesson: That is nothing that anyone can say to you, say about you, or do to you which could take away from the fact that you are a part of the greatest whole imaginable. No less than the mighty trees and the beautiful stars above, "you have a right to be here" and to be happy.

NETWORKING OR BUILDING ALLIANCES?

Carol Gallagher, PhD, wrote one of the earliest guidebooks for women in leadership in *Going to the Top*,[25] debunking the six popular myths that women believe will help them make it into the executive ranks. The myths are the beliefs that many women hold, which actually hold them back. They are:

1. The results speak for themselves.
2. You have to network to get ahead.
3. You have to be ruthless to succeed.
4. If you keep your head down, you won't get shot.
5. You need to "play the man's game" to get ahead.
6. You need to find a mentor who will pave the way for you.

Most women are surprised to see that "networking" is on the list. One of the interviewees in the book described networking as "superficial relationships or a device used to achieve a goal." Others described networking in equally manipulative terms, or more bluntly, as a "time consuming waste of energy."

Instead, Gallagher advocated the careful construction of "alliances"— building teams, attaching themselves to the right people, "collaborative work on tasks or projects," "real–ationships," creative collaborations that helped build enduring trust, and relationships that show that peers can believe in you and that you will deliver what you say you will deliver.

The alliance concept recognizes that professional relationships are not social relationships; they are organizational relationships. They are teams. There are alliances with the boss and the hierarchy above. There are horizontal alliances in addition to these vertical ones. Internal alliances exist with peers, co-workers outside of your area of functionality, and senior executives in other departments. External alliances exist among clients, professionals outside the organization, and even competitors.

To understand the difference between networking and alliances, consider what it is like to attend an event held by a professional organization. You might tend to start talking and tell everyone at the table about your business, handing out the cards you brought. Usually, every other person at the table also will be in "transmit" mode as well. Often this is called "networking," but usually little is accomplished.

Consider the person who, instead of talking about her business, seeks to genuinely understand your business—not merely what you have to offer, but also the goals you are trying to pursue. If the questioning is done well, she will know more about your firm and your interests than you will know about hers.

She gets to listen and learn where the bridges might be built between your two firms—*if* there is any opportunity to do so. She's looking for the areas where you both could benefit. How? By doing business together. She's looking for the mutual interest. Not merely *you* buying her product or *she* buying your product, today. But where could you work together to grow both of your businesses in the future, together? Where do you have common goals and objectives, and how can you increase the market for both of your products and services?

It isn't just about the business—it's also trying to determine if you are a worthy person with whom to be associated. Do you appear credible, believable, and trustworthy? Are you someone with whom it is safe to build an alliance?

Lesson: The myth of "networking" needs to be tossed out the window. In its place, learn to look for women worthy of your truly creative collaborative efforts—women who share your interests. This is "building alliances."

UNDER-EARNING

Barbara Stanny is a noted speaker, coach, and author of *Secrets of Six-Figure Women*,[26] in which she discusses the phenomenon of "women's under-earning": "To earn less than you need, or desire, for no apparent reasons and despite your efforts to do otherwise."[27]

Stanny described a cartoon from a business magazine where a group of men in suits are gathered around a conference table, and one of them is speaking. The caption reads, "Gentlemen, we need to slash expenses in half, so we're replacing each of you with a woman." Stanny noted, "What's really wrong with this picture isn't so much that the women will be offered half salary, but that the men know we'll readily accept it."[28]

Her book provides a road map out of this one-way trip to hell by tapping the advice of a host of high-earning women, including herself, based on her own experiences as a woman who lost her inheritance (her father was the R in H&R Block) through her husband's financial mismanagement.

One key element of under-earning is acceptance of one's own role in sustaining that undesired status rather than waiting for angels, princes, or other saviors (whether legislators or CEOs) to be the initiators in solving this problem. A second key element is being willing to let go of the pier in order to sail the oceans of opportunities and "six-figure" futures. Examples of successful women include those who faced the risks and uncertainties of charting their own journeys to the higher incomes they desired and, ultimately, earned.

Stanny was one of the first to document the rise in the number of women earning "six-figure incomes"—a trend that has only picked up in the twenty-first century. Her seven strategic steps to that goal tapped the wisdom of those outstanding earners, providing a road map to follow their lead:

1. Declare your intent—tell yourself you will do this.
2. Let go of the ledge—be ready to take on the opportunities.
3. Get into the game—stop hiding.
4. Speak up—voice your own ambitions.
5. Stretch—going beyond what you thought possible.
6. Seek support—know the help that you need to succeed.
7. Obey the rules of money—understand financial intelligence.

Evelyn Murphy and E. J. Graffe followed Stanny's lead with their book *Getting Even.*[29] Evelyn Murphy is president of The Wage Project Inc.,[30] and E. J. Graffe is a senior correspondent for *The American Prospect* and resident scholar at Brandeis Women's Studies Research Center. Murphy and Graffe also provide well-researched recommendations for how women can take back control of the negotiations in bidding for the salaries they deserve.

1. Document whatever unfairness you observe.
2. Do the research to learn what others (probably men) with your experience, performance record, education, or other measures get paid.
3. Collaborate with other women *and* men to reduce the risk of being ignored as a troublemaker.
4. Learn to negotiate: ask for more money and arrive at a mutually amicable price or terms.
5. Talk to the boss about a gender wage analysis.
6. Celebrate success—one woman's promotion is an achievement for all. Celebrate the achievement of simple fairness.

Lesson: The wage or salary differential is a yardstick to measure our own efforts to value our own work. What you earn is within your own control, just like the rest of your destiny.

ASSUME THE POSITION!

The scene in the cartoon *Shrek the Third** is the castle dungeon of Far Far Away. The Queen Mother Lillian, her daughter, Fiona (Shrek's wife),

---

*The 2007 computer animated film produced by DreamWorks Animation and distributed by Paramount Pictures.

and four storybook princesses are being held by a No Goodnik Prince who is planning on stealing the throne to the kingdom for himself. Every bad character in every cartoon or fantasy tale now threatens the princesses.

"What shall we do?" the fair maidens ask each other. One voice speaks up louder among them all: "Assume the position!" The four princesses go limp, begin weeping, or feign sleep or fright.

"What position?" Fiona asks.

"Waiting to be rescued, of course," replies one of the princesses.

You realize the young enchantresses have reverted to their Storybook Selves: Cinderella, Snow White, Sleeping Beauty, and Rapunzel—each waiting to be rescued by some Knight Valiant, like the true Pretty (Helpless) Women they believe themselves to be.

The Queen and Fiona will have nothing of it. Queen Mom knocks some sense into them, being the real power behind her late husband's throne. And Fiona is worthy of her leading role. They all escape thanks to the daredevil performance of these two leading cartoon ladies, with the princesses looking like Storybook Charlie's Angels at the end of the film.

So, enjoy Disney's latest film, *The Enchantress*. Remember, this is the industry that packs away $4 billion a year telling the next generation of little girls how they too can "Assume the Position!"

Lesson: In November 2010, Disney announced it would no longer be producing "princess films" because they were no longer "relevant" to young girls today. Change takes time.

ELLEN WELTY

Kudos to Ellen Welty for her article on "the cure for waffle-speak."[31] Ms. Welty cuts right to the chase by critiquing some of the most debilitating self-disparaging speaking styles that women need to eliminate from their communications.

So let's break that chain, shall we? Read on and learn how to ditch the wimpy-sounding words and phrases that may be holding you back so you can say your piece with confidence and show the world—and, really, yourself—how strong and self-possessed you truly are. *

---

*"Are Your Words Holding You Back?" by Ellen Welty, *Redbook* (a Hearst Communications publication), March 17, 2005 http://www.redbookmag.com/health-wellness/advice/words-holding-you-back

Waffle-speak includes the over-use of "like" as an empty space filler. Other self-deprecating speech patterns include the introductory "This might be stupid, but . . ." or "sorry"—words that take away from the message you are attempting to convey. Over-use of "hedging words"—"I think" or "just" or "only." The cute little-girl up-lilt at the end of sentences makes every statement sound like you're asking for permission to speak.

Ms. Welty's solutions focus on recognizing dismissive speech patterns, testing alternative assertive sentence structures, and using friends or recording devices to test out new and improved presentation styles. The challenge is to "break the chain" of "waffling and downplaying your worth. Follow this plan to banish self-defeating talk and put more me-power behind your words."

It is astounding to see such an article in the same magazine that typically blares headlines such as "How to Use Your Sexuality to Manipulate . . . [whatever!]." Ms. Welty's advice was crafted originally in March 2005.

What is *so* refreshing is to see some sincere "tough love" advice for women. This is one of the few such pieces with the courage to tell young and mature women alike how they *can* fine-tune their presentation styles and communication techniques and be heard with respect and admiration in today's marketplace. Ms. Welty speaks genuinely and truthfully on a subject too long ignored by women who have hoped they could bring their coy, little-girl ways into the adult and business world.

Lesson: You are as you speak. As more women follow Ms. Welty's suggestions, they will become more credible, more interesting, more persuasive, and more likely to succeed. That is exactly what Ms. Welty, herself, accomplished with this article.

HOW TIMES HAVE CHANGED

Dr. Lois Frankel just wrote a new book, *See Jane Lead*.[32] Dr. Frankel is best known for her *New York Times* best seller books, the *Nice Girls* series: *Nice Girls Don't Get the Corner Office* and *Nice Girls Don't Get Rich*. Her latest book truly is a reflection of more modern times. She interviewed women in leadership, asking them to discuss their insights about what they thought worked, what they did that advanced their careers, and how their perspective of leadership is appropriate to today's business challenges. It's a book that every woman should read if she is interested in being an active participant in the contemporary business marketplace.

Dr. Frankel sees the importance, now, of not looking at the things women might consider wrong in their careers but, rather, the crucial need for women to develop and strengthen strategies that will enable them to succeed at work. Dr. Frankel is very good at enumerating possible things that women *can* do to be more effective, more influential, and to be more comfortable with guiding change at work and within their careers.

Dr. Frankel is among those leaders recognizing that the masculine model of command and control in hierarchical organizations (corporate, non-profit, military, even households) is being challenged globally. What has changed are the followers. This is a new generation that responds differently. They ask "why" when given orders—they seek, first, to understand. As long-term organizational loyalties have been thrown out the window with downsizing, rightsizing, and global financial recession, the demand for new leaders is now tapping the wisdom and perspective of strong and decisive women who understand the nature of change taking place.

She sees women as "natural leaders." She also recognizes that women lead in that most basic business unit: the home, household, and family unit. She advises women to acquire some new tools, techniques, tactics, and strategies that can deliver on the promise of "natural leadership." In *See Jane Lead*, she identifies effective methods of "influence" rather than the more traditional power-based type of leadership, which is hitting its own limits in contemporary workplace environments.

Lesson: Everyone has the capacity to learn and change. Even a successful business model like the *Nice Girls* series can be remolded into a new vision for women in leadership.

ANOTHER WISE WOMAN

Dr. Elga Wasserman wrote *The Door in the Dream*[33] about the experiences of the 86 women who were elected to the National Academy of Sciences (5 percent of the total membership). As a scientist, an accomplished lawyer, and special assistant to the president of Yale University for the education of women, Dr. Wasserman wanted to know about the women who "made it" and what we could possibly learn from successful women that would help those who follow. Her book studies the women in four groups: those born before 1920, those born in the 1920s, those born in the 1930s, and those born after 1940. It's a refreshing and objective analysis.

"...We need a pool of highly trained scientists in order to maintain our role as a leading industrial nation [and] women constitute half of the talent pool."[34]

Dr. Wasserman also understands the power of "myths" to perpetuate the status quo: "Younger women internalize stereotypes that dampen their aspirations and cause them to wonder whether they belong in science at all."[35]

Dr. Wasserman was searching for what she called "shared experiences and concerns" among women of achievement that helped them to succeed. Dr. Wasserman describes her research and recommendations in the YouTube video of her June 20, 2003, Regents' Lecture at the University of California, San Diego:[36]

Shared Traits among Women in the National Academy of Sciences:

They are talented and obtained a first rate education.

Love what they do, are passionate, persistent.

Unusually optimistic, focused, energetic.

Inner-directed, nonconventional.

Able to ignore or deflect negative experiences.

Free of internal barriers and guilt.

Encountered more obstacles than their male colleagues.

Found supportive mentors.

Modest about their achievements.

Attribute their success to "luck."

Recommended Coping Strategies:

Assess your strengths, weaknesses, likes, and dislikes.

Set your own goals, pursue them, but remain flexible.

Keep in mind where you want to be in 10 years.

Don't let others decide what's best for you.

Stay focused, but don't be a perfectionist.

Keep a positive attitude. Don't dwell on setbacks; move on.

Ask for what you need. Be clear about what you have to offer.

Learn to say "no."

Use mentors wisely. Get support from colleagues, male and female.

Become visible within and beyond your institution.

Avoid hostile environments.

Find places where women have stayed and are happy. Look at critical mass, turnover, and promotion, not just hiring.

Choose a supportive mate.

Try to move to a metropolitan area with multiple employers.

Accept help with home and children.

Find a solution that is right for *you* and *your* family—one style does not fit all.

Lesson: Thank heavens for wise women.*

WOMEN IN MEDIA—HU SHULI

Who are the "outstanding" women in media? Women in the global economy are making surprising inroads into the business of publishing. Consider, for example, editor Hu Shuli of China.

Two days after leaving *Caijing*, China's leading financial news magazine, editor Hu reportedly accepted an offer to become dean of the School of Communication and Design at Zhongshan University (Sun Yat-Sen University) in Guangzhou (the province formerly known as Canton) in southern China, near Hong Kong.

Earlier in 2010, Ms. Hu set up her own publishing company, *Caixin Media*, to produce a weekly magazine (now called *Century Weekly*) and books and to organize conferences.

Caixin Media is a periodical licensed to the China Institute for Reform and Development in Haikou, capital of Hainan province (one of 9,500 licensed periodicals in the country).

Ms. Hu's first issue of *Century Weekly* was welcomed by the *Wall Street Journal* blog, *China Real Time Report*.[37] The inaugural issue of *Century Weekly* focused on inflation, corruption, and "reshuffling executives at banks as a way to address governance problems."

Where in the United States is there any comparable woman in media willing to take on the substantive governance issues, lead a major profit-oriented media enterprise, and speak out on contemporary financial issues?

Lesson: Those who hold the pen write the story.

---

*Excerpts reprinted with permission from *The Door in the Dream*, 2000, by the National Academy of Sciences, Courtesy of the National Academies Press, Washington, D.C.

SIX

In Politics: Women Who Are Political Change Agents

Role models are mentors. When women "see" another woman in leadership, she can envision herself in a similar position. The best example of this is when we remember the words of Vigdís Finnbogadóttir (the first female president of Iceland, serving from 1980 to 1996). After her first eight years in office as Iceland's president, she said that some youngsters in her country thought that you *had* to be a woman to hold the office.

Until Barack Obama became the first African American president of the United States, we assumed that only white males could hold that leadership position. Until Mary Barra was named as chief executive officer of General Motors, we expected that auto-industry leadership would not be held by a woman engineer. Perhaps "firsts" are necessary. They need not be "only."

Women who succeed in the political medium clearly have had to serve as their own mentors. The women who have achieved political leadership are both few and incredibly outstanding. They have accomplished this on a very public stage, on the merits of their experience and careers, which is why they are such powerful role models.

We can look back at some of the early years of women's struggles to be elected both at the state and federal levels. We can learn from their actions, writings, advice, and insight. Political leaders are public servants, providing us with solutions to shared biases, barriers, and obstacles. But before they can help us, they have to overcome their own challenges and take office.

MOMENTUM

Ronna Romney was twice a Republican candidate for U.S. senator from Michigan (unsuccessfully). In 1994, she lost in the primary to Spencer Abraham (who served from 1994 to 2000). She lost in the 1996 general election to Senator Carl Levin (a six-term incumbent from 1978 to 2008). She married into a prominent Republican political family. She is the ex-wife of G. Scott Romney (son of Michigan governor George W. Romney and brother of Massachusetts governor and presidential candidate Mitt Romney). Ms. Romney was a member of the Republican National Committee from 1984 to 1992.[1]

Ronna Romney knows politics, which is one reason she wrote a handbook for women political candidates: *Momentum: Women in American Politics Now*, written with Beppie Harrison.[2] *Momentum* is a book that doesn't lose credibility with time.

Eight simple chapters cover all the essential topics that we saw as recently as the Hillary Clinton campaign in 2007–2008. We still register astonishment at the challenges Ms. Clinton faced, showing that we have not yet understood the lessons and insight contained in Romney and Harrison's book.

To summarize the lessons from each chapter:

1. "Banners, Bunting, and All That"—why women (just like men) love the political process
2. "Hitting the Hurdles"—you thought this would be easy?
3. "The Campaign Trail"—politics, legislation, and sausages, none of them pretty
4. "The Money Game"—essentials, dearie, essentials
5. "Women among Men"—what it's really like on the inside
6. "Other Women"—sometimes, even more brutal
7. "Where Do We Get to from Here?"—more quo vadis: learn, baby, learn

Romney and Harrison describe three stages to women's political development:[3]

- . . .the first being the hopeless, stubborn races where the woman is jeered at as a fool and as a shame to her sex;
- the second being the stage in which a very few women are accepted as anomalies in the system, but always as the exceptions to the normal rules; and

- the third being the nirvana in which a woman candidate expects, and gets, matter-of-fact-acceptance as a candidate depending on her qualifications. . . .

Where are we, now, and where are we going? In 1988, when Romney and Harrison wrote *Momentum*, they thought we probably were "somewhere between stage two and stage three. . . ." On today's campaign trail, we can see evidence of all three stages spread across the nation, because not all communities have demonstrated the same levels of education, or social or political maturity. The difference today is the sheer number of women who are either running for, or are being appointed to, extremely responsible positions of political leadership where they are acquiring the right experience and qualifications to take on the very top leadership positions.

But progress has happened. As one example, in 2000, Spencer Abraham was defeated for a second term in the Senate by Debbie Stabenow (D-MI). A more recent example is the leadership of Senate Budget Committee chair Patty Murray (a four-term senator from Washington), who co-brokered the late 2014 budget deal with Rep. Paul Ryan, preventing repeat of a potentially disastrous government shutdown. Sometimes, political success just takes time.

In 2014, Ronna Romney's daughter, Ronna Romney McDaniel, was elected to the Republican National Committee after an activist career supporting Republican candidates in the latest presidential campaign and service on the GOP state committee. They are the first mother and daughter to serve in this leadership capacity from Michigan. Many consider McDaniel to be a rising star in the party—at the state level and perhaps nationally.

Lesson: In order to earn the "matter-of-fact acceptance" as a political candidate, women have had to traverse the two tougher stages of evolution. They are now out there on the playing field, the political stage, and the campaign trail. This is the meaning of "momentum."

WOMEN IN U.S. POLITICAL LEADERSHIP

We seem upset when Catalyst Inc. or another women's advocacy network informs us that "there are *only*" 15 percent or 16 percent or 17 percent women among some top leadership group: boards of directors, CEOs, CFOs, or some other C-level position.

The advocates typically allege that "it's all their fault"—those pale, stale males who are keeping all the women out of the top leadership opportunities. But what about that great level playing field, the American political marketplace? The same percentages exist for women in leadership along the political path. If less than a fifth of that marketplace are women, then isn't that more a reflection of the society and the culture (the voter marketplace) in which we live rather than the domination of only half over the other?

If women wanted other women to be in political leadership, wouldn't they be likely to support other women who pursue and achieve positions of leadership? If women control or influence 80 to 90 percent of our consumer dollars, don't they also have the power to channel funds in support of their half of the campaign marketplace?

According to the U.S. 2010 Census, women represent 52 percent of the total population, 53 percent of registered voters, and 53 percent of voter turnout.[4] The voter turnout of women has outpaced that of men by at least 5 million voters every presidential election since 1980. According to Rutgers University's Center for American Women and Politics (CAWP), in 2008, the "gender gap" was 9.7 million women voters more than male voters.[5] So, it would appear that all women needed to do was to show up and vote on election day. But not all women vote for women. So we end up with just about the same percentage share of women in political leadership as we have in corporate leadership. Perhaps, today, this is the level of evolution of women's support of women in leadership.

As of 2014, 18.4 percent (or 249) of the nation's 1,351 mayors (of cities larger than 30,000 population) are women.[6] Another 24.2 percent (1,784) of all 7,383 state legislators are women.[7] Ninety-nine women (18.5 percent of the total of 535 seats) serve in Congress. Twenty (20 percent) are senators and 79 (18.2 percent) are representatives. The percentages are surprisingly consistent across business and politics.[8]

The first congresswoman, Jeannette Rankin (R-MT), took office in 1917. Nancy Landon Kassenbaum (R-KS) was the first woman elected to the Senate in 1922. From those early beginnings to today, there have been a whopping 33 women senators. Another 251 women representatives have served in the House. Ten women have served in both houses, and four women were named delegates to the House.[9]

As of 2013, five women serve among the 50 possible gubernatorial positions in the United States. Altogether, there have been 35 women governors from 26 states (20 Democrats and 15 Republicans) since the first one held office in 1924. Most of today's current crop came into office after 1967–1968. Twenty-three women were elected in their own right; eight became governor when the elected governor left office for one reason or another, three replaced their spouses, and one woman was governor of Puerto Rico.[10]

Looking at our political landscape, it appears that women are just beginning to take political leadership seriously enough to campaign on an equal footing with their peers. Historically, women tended to identify with minor party issues, typically dealing with limited labor or feminist political planks. The likelihood of getting into office following that route is somewhere between small and none.

Being a woman in leadership is an exceptional undertaking that only about 17 to 20 percent of the marketplace (women) appear willing to pursue. Rather than focus on all of those "old boys" whom some women argue are keeping women out of leadership positions, perhaps it really is time we started to look at two other far more important factors:

1. Who *are* the women who constitute that 17 to 20 percent of leadership in contemporary society and culture? How did they pursue it? How did they achieve it? How could other women emulate them?

2. Why is it that society and culture (or bias and discrimination) failed so miserably at keeping those women back, behind, and out of leadership positions when those demons have been so successful at keeping the other 80 to 83 percent "in their place"?

Lesson: Perhaps we should focus on the top tier of women in political leadership a little more and stop listening to the bottom tier altogether.

WOMEN U.S. CABINET MEMBERS

The fact that 44 percent of current U.S. cabinet members are women (seven out of sixteen) demonstrates that it is more likely that talented women will be appointed to a position of political leadership based on their expertise than that they will achieve it by the election process. Throughout history, we have had 52 women hold cabinet-level positions, 30 named by Democrats and 22 by Republicans.[11]

More women have headed up the Department of Labor (seven) than any other cabinet post.

- Frances Perkins (1933–1945)—Franklin D. Roosevelt
- Ann Dore McLaughlin (1987–1989)—Ronald Reagan
- Elizabeth Dole (1989–1990)—George H.W. Bush
- Lynn M. Martin (1991–1993)—George H.W. Bush
- Alexis Herman (1997–2001)—Bill Clinton

- Elaine Cho (2001–2009)—George W. Bush
- Hilda Solis (2009–)—Barack Obama

Six women have headed the Environmental Protection Agency (EPA, including one in a brief acting capacity). The EPA was founded in 1970, and while it is not officially a cabinet department, the administrator has been given cabinet rank.

- Anne M. Burford (1981–1983)—Ronald Reagan
- Carol M. Browner (1993–2001)—Bill Clinton
- Christine Todd Whitman (2001–2003)—George W. Bush
- Marianne Lamont Horinko (acting, 2003)—George W. Bush
- Gina McCarthy (2013–)—
- Lisa P. Jackson (2009–2013)—Barack Obama
- Gina McCarthy (2013–)—Barack Obama

Five women have headed the Department of Health and Human Services:

- Patricia Roberts Harris (1979–1981)—Jimmy Carter
- Margaret Heckler (1983–1985)—Ronald Reagan
- Donna Shalala (1993–2001)—Bill Clinton
- Kathleen Sebelius (2009–2014)—Barack Obama
- Sylvia Matthews Burwell (2014–) Barack Obama

In 1979, the Department of Health, Education and Welfare (HEW) was split into the Department of Health and Human Services (HHS) and the Department of Education. Patricia Roberts Harris was the last secretary of HEW (1979) and the first secretary of HHS (1979–1981). She also served as Secretary of Housing and Urban Development (1977–1979). All of her appointments were made by Jimmy Carter. Oveta Culp Hobby (1953–1955) was appointed by Dwight Eisenhower as the first head of the Department of Health, Education and Welfare.

Four women have headed the Department of Commerce:

- Juanita A. Kreps (1977–1979)—Jimmy Carter
- Barbara H. Franklin (1992–1993)—George H.W. Bush
- Rebecca Blank (acting, 2011–2013)—Barack Obama
- Penny Pritzker (2013–)—Barack Obama

Three women have headed the Department of Transportation:

- Elizabeth Dole (1983–1985)—Ronald Reagan
- Maria Cino (acting 2006)—George W. Bush
- Mary E. Peters (2006–2009)—George W. Bush

Three women have headed the State Department:

- Madeleine K. Albright (1997–2001)—Bill Clinton
- Condoleezza Rice (2005–2009)—George W. Bush
- Hillary Rodham Clinton (2009–2013)—Barack Obama

Two women each have headed the Departments of Education, Housing and Urban Development, and Interior:

Education:

- Shirley Mount Hufstedler (1979–1981)—Jimmy Carter
- Margaret Spellings (2005–2009)—George W. Bush

Housing and Urban Development:

- Carla Anderson Hills (1975–1977)—Gerald Ford
- Patricia Roberts Harris (1977–1979)—Jimmy Carter

Interior:

- Gale A. Norton (2001–2006)—George W. Bush
- Sally Jewell (2013–)—Barack Obama

One woman each has headed Agriculture, Energy, Attorney General, and Homeland Security:

- Agriculture: Ann M. Veneman (2001–2005)—George W. Bush
- Energy: Hazel O'Leary (1993–2001)—Bill Clinton
- Attorney General: Janet Reno (1993–2001)—Bill Clinton
- Homeland Security: Janet Napolitano (2009–2013)—Barack Obama

Four women have been U.S. trade representatives:

- Carla Anderson Hills (1989–1993)—George H.W. Bush
- Charlene Barshefsky (1997–2001)—Bill Clinton
- Susan Schwab (2006–2009)—George W. Bush
- Susan Rice (2009–)—Barack Obama

Eight women have been named as head of the Small Business Administration (SBA), although three of them have held the position of acting administrator.

- Susan Engeleiter (1989–1991)—George H.W. Bush
- Pat Saiki (1991–1993)—George H.W. Bush
- Cassandra M. Pulley (acting, 1994)—Bill Clinton
- Ginger Lew (acting, 1997)—Bill Clinton
- Aída Álvarez (1997–2001)—Bill Clinton
- Karen Mills (2009–2013)—Barack Obama
- Jeanne Hulit (acting 2013–2014)—Barack Obama
- Maria Contreras-Sweet (confirmed March 27, 2014)—Barack Obama

Contreras-Sweet is the only woman administrator who is also the founder of a bank and has extensive experience with SBA lending to entrepreneurs.[12]

Alice M. Rivlin (1994–1996) was the first woman to serve as head of the Office of Management and Budget (OMB), appointed by Bill Clinton. Sylvia Mathews Burwell was appointed director of the OMB by President Barack Obama in 2013.

Christina Romer was chair of the Council of Economic Advisors under Barack Obama (2009–2010). Laura D'Andrea Tyson served on the Council of Economic Advisors (1993–1995) and the National Economic Council (1995–1996) under Bill Clinton. Janet L. Yellen was on the Council of Economic Advisors (1997–1999) under Bill Clinton and became the first woman appointed to head the Federal Reserve System and chair its board of governors in 2013, nominated by Barack Obama. Anne Armstrong was named counsellor to the president by Nixon and then Ford (1973–1974).

Barack Obama named 18 women to top-level positions; Bill Clinton named 13; George W. Bush named 10; George H.W. Bush named 6; Jimmy Carter named 5, and Ronald Reagan named 4. Richard Nixon, Gerald Ford, Dwight Eisenhower, and Franklin D. Roosevelt each named one woman. John F. Kennedy did not name any women to a cabinet or executive advisory position.

Women have not yet been named to head Defense, Veterans Affairs, or Treasury. However, Susan Morrisey Livingstone was an acting U.S. Secretary of the Navy (in the Defense Department) in the George W. Bush administration for two months in 2003.

A significant number of these political leaders went on to become directors at one or more corporations. The first time the National Association of Corporate Directors (NACD) awarded its Director of the Year distinction (1987), they gave it to Juanita Kreps, former secretary of commerce. Barbara Franklin is the past chair of the NACD. Laura Tyson was tapped by the British to examine best practices to promote diversity among UK nonexecutive directors. Patricia Roberts Harris was the first woman and first African American named a director to a major U.S. corporation, IBM, in 1971. Carla Hills, Charlene Barshefsky, Susan Schwab, Elizabeth Dole, and Shirley Hufstedler all continue to serve on multiple boards.

Lesson: Elected and appointed positions in the political field offer an entire generation an opportunity to observe how well women perform as role models, leaders, and mentors on the public stage.

EMILY CARD

Samantha thought that finally she had "made it" on her own merits. She'd finished college, worked at a great job for a couple of years, made some "adult" investments like a car and a stereo—her first journey into the scary world of credit. She saved her money as well because she wanted to go to business school and knew that that would be pricey.

The economy was not doing well in the early 1970s—stagflation mixed the worst of both stagnant economic growth and inflation. Samantha decided it might be smart to take some time off work to go to B-school and see if the economy could right itself by the time she finished.

She took an accelerated program, nevertheless, hoping to get back into her career path as soon as possible. Samantha was very proud that she'd managed the financing of her degree program well. She'd received work-study grants thanks to the generous recommendations of two of the department's top professors. They also had been instrumental in her receiving research awards that included small stipends from professional associations in her field of study. And she had tapped the federal loan fund that was available to graduate students. Samantha made a promise to herself that, when she graduated, she would pay back that loan, unlike many of her peers who simply bailed on their federal loan obligations. She thought the repayment terms were very generous and more than reasonable.

Samantha graduated, got a great job, was paying back her loan, had a steady and growing income, and even managed to get a credit card in her own name. Being fiscally conservative, Samantha chose to use the card only rarely until she'd paid back her student loan.

When Samantha met the man who would be her husband, all seemed right with the world. He admired and respected her self-sufficiency, and she was amazed by both his worldliness and his caring. As they considered moving in together, life's petty details hit them by surprise.

First, Samantha's fiscal independence would be history if they were married. She would no longer be able to hold a credit card in her own name. Even her Macy's shopping card would have to be traded in if she took his name.

If they decided to avoid this problem by "just living together," their auto insurance company told them their rates would at least double, if not more, because they were choosing to live in "an untraditional arrangement" according to the social standards of the seventies.

Thank heaven that Emily W. Card also was upset at the barriers to credit faced by married women. It smacked of those days when women were considered literally "the property of their spouses"—an ancient concept at best. The modern equivalent of economic slavery at its worst.

Emily Card was a U.S. Senate fellow when she researched, drafted, and floor managed the 1973 Senate passage of the Equal Credit Opportunity Act. The House passed it in 1974, and President Gerald Ford signed it in October 1974.[13] As an aide to Senator William Brock (R-TN), she was liaison to women's groups that helped build evidence of discrimination and support for the Act. That legislation outlawed credit discrimination based on sex or marital status.

Emily Card, PhD, JD, and MPA, founded the Women's Credit Project while she was a faculty member at the University of Southern California; founded the Women's Credit and Finance Project at Harvard University; wrote a weekly column on finance for *Ms.* magazine; hosted a cable television program on financial advice for women; published a total of seven books on consumer finance, including *Staying Solvent: Comprehensive Guide to Equal Credit for Women*; and was a visiting professor of law in the LLM program at the Instituto Tecnologico de Monterrey (TEC de Monterrey) in Mexico.[14]

Samantha often wonders to herself what the last four decades might have looked like if women did not have the ability to have credit in their own names.

Lesson: Sometimes we take our most important mentors for granted.

PATSY T. MINK

Title IX of the Education Amendments of 1972[15] was authored by Birch Bayh (D-IN) in the Senate and Patsy Takemoto Mink (D-HA) in the House of Representatives. The legislation prohibits gender discrimination in "any educational program or activity" that receives federal funding and today carries the name the Patsy T. Mink Equal Opportunity in Education Act of 1972.

Patsy Mink experienced discrimination at the University of Nebraska first hand and challenged the status quo with a collaboration of students, teachers, and activists.[16] She studied pre-medicine as an undergraduate at the University of Hawaii at Honolulu but could not get accepted at any medical school in 1948 because of discrimination against women. She applied and was accepted at the University of Chicago Law School, graduating with a juris doctor degree in 1951. She used the law to challenge bias against women in education throughout her impressive legislative career.

She served in the Hawaii Territorial House of Representatives in 1956–1958, was a member of the Hawaii Territorial Senate from 1958–1959, and a member of the Hawaii State Senate from 1962–1964.

She served in the U.S. Congress from 1965–1977 and again from 1990 until her death in 2002. She was a candidate for president, running in the Oregon primary in 1972 on an anti-war platform during the Vietnam War era. She was the first Asian American to run for the U.S. presidency.

In the 1960s, Representative Mink initiated legislation creating federal programs and funding to support early childhood education (pre-school through kindergarten). She introduced the Women's Educational Equity Act of 1974, which provided competitive grants for local initiatives supporting gender equality and the advancement of women's education opportunities. The Bush administration terminated the act's Equity Resource Center in 2003, and later administrations have cut funding for both initiatives.

Her most significant legislation was and is Title IX, but even that law has been challenged numerous times in the courts and in the halls of Congress.

Lesson: Legislative support of equal treatment for women and prohibitions on gender discrimination are essential. It is not enough that great minds like Patsy Mink create such innovative legislation. It takes generations of support afterward to ensure that these rights remain intact.

BROOKSLEY BORN

Brooksley Born probably is doing more today to change our views and oversight of financial risk and derivative instruments than ever before in her incredible career, yet there was never anyone more overlooked when she should have been heeded.

Brooksley Born is a graduate of Stanford University and Stanford Law School (1961, JD 1964), and a (retired in 2003) partner at Arnold & Porter, where she was head of the firm's derivatives practice. A recent article about her in the *Stanford Alumni Magazine* provides an interesting overview of her background and cases.

One of seven women in the Class of 1964 at Stanford Law School, she graduated at the top of her class, and was elected president of the law review, the first woman to hold either distinction. She is credited with being the first woman to edit a major American law review.[17]

She was named by President Bill Clinton as chair of the Commodity Futures Trading Commission (CFTC) in August 1996 and served until June 1999. Her most prominent work at the CFTC was a draft "concept release" that tried to tackle the emerging complexities of over-the-counter (OTC) derivatives.

The press release introducing the Concept Release on May 7, 1998,[18] warned that the notional value of derivatives had reached more than "$28 trillion worldwide" and that these were essentially unregulated. "While OTC derivatives serve important economic functions, these products, like any complex financial instrument, can present significant risks if misused or misunderstood." The notional value of derivatives rose to over $600 trillion by 2007.

The CFTC Concept Release provided 75 questions that needed to be addressed before undertaking OTC derivatives regulation.[19] Most of these questions remain unanswered even today, 15 years and one Great Financial Crisis later.

Brooksley Born testified before a Congressional House committee discussing the pros and cons of different approaches to derivatives regulation in July 1998.[20] In October 23, 1998, she testified on the impact of technology on the regulation of derivatives markets and lessons from the failure of Long Term Capital Management.[21]

In 2009, she was honored with the John F. Kennedy Profile in Courage Award along with Sheila Bair (then head of the Federal Deposit Insurance Corp.), Senator Edward M. Kennedy (D-MA), and Leymah Gbowee (representing the Women of Liberia's Mass Action for Peace).[22]

A recent *Washington Post* interview with Brooksley Born shows her continuing graciousness. Even though she probably foresaw the oncoming train wreck that was the financial crash of 2007, she is not so politically naïve as to say, "You were warned." Today, she is in greater demand for her financial insight than ever before.[23]

Most recently, she was named by Speaker Nancy Pelosi to be one of ten members of the Financial Crisis Inquiry Commission (FCIC) headed by Phil Angelides, chartered by Congress in May 2009 (through February 2011), to examine the causes of the worst financial crisis since the Great Depression.[24] The FCIC was authorized by Congress[25] and given a shopping list of the possible sources of the recent financial disaster and bailout. Significant among those causes, certainly, was the failure to regulate OTC derivatives.

Now in 2013, Brooksley Born is warning about the risks of banks that are "too big to fail" and that will require massive federal bailouts when (not if) they do.[26]

Lesson: Perhaps we should be listening to this woman.

SANDRA DAY O'CONNOR

The highest public office in the United States is the lifetime appointment to the Supreme Court, a position achieved by Sandra Day O'Connor as the first woman Supreme Court justice in 1981 (retiring in 2006).

How did a young cattle-ranching girl from the Arizona-New Mexico border grow up to become the first woman nominated as justice of the U.S. Supreme Court? What does that background tell us about the basis for her judicial thinking?

Sandra Day O'Connor wrote *Lazy B: Growing Up on a Cattle Ranch in the American Southwest*,[27] with her brother H. Alan Day, as a tribute to their parents, the men who worked the ranch with them, and the rustic, hardscrabble ethos of the desert ranch life.

Through Sandra and Alan's eyes, you meet their parents, Mo (Ada Mae) and Da (Harry) Day, Alan's twin sister (Ann), Sandra's friends, and the ranch hands whose mores match those of Da and who passed those values onto Sandra.

The people whose lives most guided her perspective on the world were rough and tough gentlemen: Rafael Estrada, Jim Brister, Claude Tippets, Ira Johnson, Lehoy McCarty, Cole Webb, and Ralph (Bug) Quinn. "There was never a day without things that needed doing," said Sandra. The chapters are filled with the manner and style by which they accomplished every task.

A most memorable chapter describes the time when she, just home from her junior high school year at El Paso, Texas, volunteered to be "Bug's

Stand-In" as cook.[28] She offered to take the lunches prepared by her mother out to the crew at the cattle branding and roundup site: a trek of two and a half hours by truck over the hot desert terrain on unpaved road—"more a track than a road," actually. Her introduction to that chapter reads: "A job doesn't get done when it's started with a promise and finished with an alibi."[29]

Maybe an hour after starting out, the truck began wobbling, and she realized it had a flat tire. There was no AAA to call for a tow, nobody to text message for help, not even an instruction manual in the glove compartment. "If the tire was to be changed, I had to do it."

She must have watched her father change numerous flat tires and methodically followed what she'd seen him do. Place some rocks under the other set of wheels to keep the truck from rolling. Find the spare tire, the jack, and the lug wrench. Place the jack under the axle near the flat tire, pump the jack until the tire is off the ground. But here she encountered challenges her father probably had not faced. He was physically much stronger than she and capable of leveraging the lug nuts loose. She was just a teenager, not conditioned by decades on the range. "I could get no purchase on the nut." She had no leverage: the tire just spun around as she struggled to loosen the heavily rusted lug nuts.

She decided she needed to lower the jack until the weight of the tire on the ground provided the necessary resistance. Even with that, she had to stand on the lug wrench and ply it with her entire weight to accomplish the goal. "Joy! It worked!"

After removing all five rusted-tight nuts in the same manner, she re-elevated the truck axle, removed and replaced the spent tire, tightened the nuts by hand, then lowered the axle to attain the resistance of the ground again, where she could secure the nuts with the wrench, and finally lower the truck axle back down. She packed all the equipment away and proceeded to meet the crew.

She had started at 7:00 a.m. and arrived at the work site at 11:00 a.m. after an hour's delay fixing the flat. She made the cook fire and the coffee and unloaded the lunch for the crew—just as Bug Quinn would have done had he been there.

"I had expected a word of praise for changing the tire. But, to the contrary, I realized that only one thing was expected: an on-time lunch. No excuses accepted."

She remembers the day of the flat tire vividly because, much later that same evening, the family watched from their porch what turned out to be the first atomic bomb test, 180 miles away at Alamogordo, New Mexico (July 16, 1945).

"The world we knew was changed forever."

Sandra Day O'Connor graduated from Stanford University with a BA in economics and from Stanford Law School at the top of her class. Private law firms would not hire her, so she turned to a career in public law, then state government, where she served in all three branches. Thirty-six years later, in the summer of 1981, President Ronald Reagan named this "ranch girl" as a justice of the Supreme Court of the United States In *Lazy B*, she doesn't even mention the fact that she was the first woman on the bench. She served on the top federal bench for 24 years.

Justice O'Connor's life is an affirmation of personal responsibility and accountability. Once a person takes a step in any direction, one must be prepared to take full and complete ownership of all the possible consequences of that step—the good news and the bad news. No one but yourself is responsible for your choices. "No excuses accepted."

Lesson: The story of Sandra Day O'Connor's young life certainly shines a different light upon the woman in the dark robe, upon all of the choices that every woman must make, and upon all of the consequences of choices made by this nation since that day in the south-central part of New Mexico, now 53 years ago.[30]

WHAT DOES SHE MEAN?

What did Supreme Court Justice nominee Sonia Sotomayor mean when she said that different experiences count for something? Perhaps she is suggesting that we are a richer society because we are compelled to consider the impact of our divergent perspectives on a wide array of audiences. We have an obligation at least to listen.

Our forefathers and mothers fled isolated isles, countries, and continents because there was not enough room there to accommodate different thoughts and ideas. First sons, by the rule of primogeniture, inherited the world. Second and subsequent sons and their brides came to our shores to exercise freedom of religion, speech, and economic choice.

Today, the search for a field of play that is open and inviting continues. The media princes who would pre-judge this capable candidate before she has her rightful hour upon the hearing stage—the due process of the Senate confirmation review proceedings—are no better than the princes of common law in ancient England and Europe who would have shut down all dissent about "their right to rule."

Lesson: At least we can listen.

IS AMERICA READY FOR A FEMALE LEADER?

There have been 36 women who sought to be a candidate for the office of the U.S. presidency, including Hillary Clinton's 2008 campaign as a Democrat. The list also includes Gracie Allen in 1940 and Roseanne Barr in 2012—hardly serious candidates. Most female presidential candidates represented marginal or non-major parties such as the People's Party, Right to Life, Peace and Freedom, Socialist, Social Equity, Socialist Workers, Workers' World, American, Looking Back, Independent, Equal Rights, National Equal Rights, New Alliance, Citizens, Green, and the Communist Party. Only nine women were contenders from one of the two majority parties: three were Republican and six were Democratic candidates.[31]

Margaret Chase Smith (1964)—R

Shirley Anita Chisholm (1972)—D

Patsy Takemoto Mink (1972)—D

Ellen McCormack (1976, 1980)—D

Patricia S. Schroeder (1988)—D

Elizabeth Hanford Dole (2000)—R

Carol Moseley Braun (2004)—D

Hillary Rodham Clinton (2008)—D

Michele Bachmann (2012)—R

Most of these women did not make it past the preliminaries. Margaret Chase Smith was the first woman to have her name placed in nomination by a major U.S. party. She lost all of the primaries but came in fifth in the initial voter tally. In 1972, Shirley Chisholm was the first African American candidate, and Patsy Mink was the first Asian American candidate for president but lost most of the primaries to George McGovern. She won 152 delegate votes in the Democratic Convention—more than any woman candidate. Ellen McCormack ran twice on a pro-life platform but won no primaries. Pat Schroeder didn't really become a candidate, just suggested she might. Elizabeth Dole pulled out before the primaries of 2000. Carol Moseley-Braun ran for 11 months but withdrew before the Iowa caucuses. Michele Bachmann ran for 11 months then withdrew after coming in sixth in the Iowa caucuses. Hillary Clinton won far more primaries and delegates than any other female candidate in American history but conceded the nomination to Barack Obama, who went on to win the national election in 2008, just days before the Democratic Convention.

One of the few shows on prime time television, with at least one and often two women political commentators, is Chris Matthews's *Hardball*. These women political analysts are not airheads. They are intelligent women with experience and the talent to conduct meaningful research and interviews with today's top issue leaders. They are not trying to get into the "feelings" of their subjects: they pursue the subject from an informed and educated perspective. It is *such* a relief to listen to smart women present themselves effectively.

Another reason to watch the show is that they actually discuss subjects that we should be addressing as a nation, not merely pander to the lowest possible common denominator of political correctness.

Twice now, Chris Matthews has broached that forbidden subject and given it the fresh air of deliberation: "Is America ready for a female leader?" Is this mature, educated, so-called sophisticated democracy ready, willing, and able to do something that many nations of the world have done for some time now?

Gloria Arroyo, president of the Philippines

Michelle Bachelet, president of Chile

Helen Clark, prime minister of New Zealand

Luisa Diogo, prime minister of Mozambique

Tarja Halonen, president of Finland

Han Myung-sook, prime minister of South Korea

Mary McAleese, president of Ireland

Angela Merkel, chancellor of Germany

Portia Simpson Miller, prime minister of Jamaica

Vaira Vike-Freiberga, president of Latvia

Wu Yi, vice premier of China

Khaleda Zia, prime minister of Bangladesh

Let's also not forget Golda Meir (Israel), Margaret Thatcher (England), and Vigdís Finnbogadóttir (Iceland).

When we mention the prospect of a female leader, the typical response in America today, is "Don't you mean are we ready for *the right* female leader?" presenting that old double standard where we have elected both inexperienced and incompetent male presidential candidates, but we have to have the *perfect* female if we're going to have any female leader at all.

John F. Kennedy, as a U.S. senator in 1956, put this bias into clear perspective when he described the attributes he thought the first woman U.S. president would have to possess:

. . . the first woman president, because of the fact that she is a woman, will have to be an extraordinarily capable chief executive. She will require the charm and wisdom of an Eleanor Roosevelt, the leadership and military prowess of a Joan of Arc, the stately compassion of a Queen Victoria, the political sagacity of a Clare Boothe Luce, the courageous determination of a Sister Kenny, the pluck "to keep going under almost overwhelming odds" of a Helen Keller and, in addition, all of the best qualifications and skills of the Republican and Democratic lady officials mentioned earlier in this article. No doubt beauty and grace will also be important to her nomination and her election.[32]

Not only does the "perfect woman" bias pervade the political debate almost six decades later, but our female leaders have become magnets for criticism that never would be applied to any male. Who cares if Condoleezza Rice is or is not married? Does or does not play the piano? Wears one brand of shoes or another? The American public cares more about these matters than it cares about whether or not she is keeping the Middle East dialog going while Nero fiddles in the Oval Office.

Matthews has done something that no other broadcast has dared to do: considered Senator Hillary Rodham Clinton as a presidential candidate on the same basis as the other candidates (all male, obviously). How rare! They looked at the organization she assembled, her ability to attract campaign funding, her timing, her recent positions and presentations. They concluded the obvious—that she should have the Democratic Party nomination and the election, if all things were equal. But, categorically, all things are not equal.

Two different groups of Matthews's commentators concluded that America is more ready for a black president than it is for a female president. At least that conclusion is consistent with historic trends. Blacks earned their freedom before women did. Blacks got the vote before women did. Blacks were named to the Supreme Court and elected to Congress and other political positions of power before women. So it is not surprising that Barack Obama attracted so much attention as a presidential candidate, even winning the exclusive endorsement of America's daytime television maven, Oprah Winfrey—perhaps his most key endorsement. America was more prepared to accept a black leader than a female leader. That was a journey we had to take, but now having past that hurdle, today we must understand why hesitations might persist about selecting a woman president.

The reaction of contemporaries to Senator Clinton is highly reminiscent of the attitudes of our mothers' generation's antipathy toward Eleanor Roosevelt, who often was characterized as uppity, arrogant, and aggressive in her day. You'd think we'd have learned something in the past seventy years.

Perhaps we have learned something about prejudice—about pre-judging people based on their appearances, their looks, or any other short-cuts that let us avoid the really hard challenge of getting to know a person as an individual—for who he or she are and what they represent as a human. We've learned, again from those who have experienced the unfairness of our pre-judging, that we must constantly resist old tendencies, old social-ization, and old biases because these things do not just go away easily of their own accord. Barack Obama today has benefited from the lessons of old biases. We must challenge our pre-judging and prejudices head on if we want to stop the knee-jerk tendency to dismiss a person—a woman—prematurely before we truly know who she is and what she has to offer.

I would wish that America in the twenty-first century could look at a female candidate for president as if she were an equal human being in ev-ery respect. I fear that we are not there yet. I see women look up at a fe-male candidate, feel jealousy and envy, and therefore attempt to bring her down to their lower level of self-esteem—to re-establish their comfort level. I do not see women today look up to our female leaders with admira-tion and respect. Until women are willing to do that, we will not have earned the right to follow female leaders wherever they may take us.

Before we can follow them, we must first ensure that we have done the best that we can to cleanse ourselves of the biases and prejudices that limit our own potential. That means that we have to be willing to look at our attitudes toward our current and potential female leaders. Jack Kennedy made us stand up and stare at our bias and prejudice against a Catholic president. Barack Obama made us look at our prejudices against blacks. Hillary Clinton has to make us stand up and face the reality of our pre-conceived notions about a female leader.

Lesson: At every major historical juncture, the challenge of potential change appears huge and nearly insurmountable. Once we have scaled that cliff by our conscious choice and look back, we are astounded that we once considered it such an intimidating obstacle.

SEVEN

In Memoriam: Mentors Who Are No Longer with Us and Their Lessons

The saddest lesson from mentors is the realization that they are no longer with us. That does not prevent us from learning from their lives and their stories.

Newspaper headlines and obituaries alike show us great women mentors who may have passed on, but their lessons are etched in our lives and our memories. Some women may be famous, but more likely, we have not heard their stories because they were quiet, purposeful, and humble leaders doing the things that interested them, but doing that incredibly well.

Writers have been trying to teach us how to avoid or overcome the stressors that seem, inevitably, to weigh more heavily on the shoulders of working women. We can almost see them talking to us, trying to tell us to heed their advice.

The past four decades have made the most significant impact on the ways women look at themselves and their careers, and more importantly, how others view modern women as partners in business, banking, the law, manufacturing, and trade. It was a woman who gave us the Copyright Protection Act, created an innovative financial literacy program, and whose creative research led to an unprecedented Nobel Prize in Economics.

Many other valued mentors (mothers, family members, teachers, employers, authors, and researchers) may be gone, but their lessons are written carefully in our hearts and minds. Thank heaven.

A LITTLE MORE FROM GINGER

A professor friend once suggested that books dealing with the subject of women in leadership should be written from the perspective of how women compare to men as executives. What were the differences? Are we really interested only in knowing how women did what men did? Or might we learn something new and different by focusing on what the women did themselves?

A book is real estate. Like a farm, every square yard can be planted with something that might grow. If you split the crop between two types of seed in order to allocate space 50/50 to the comparison of women to men, then half of the stories and half of the experiences have to be given over to the men. That would mean that women would get less space devoted to the description of how they became executives or leaders in their enterprises and how they viewed their careers and accomplishments.

Worse, it actually ends up giving the women even less space and attention because, inevitably, there would be many words and paragraphs devoted to how or why women were "different from men" rather than focusing on how and why women did exactly what they did and accomplished exactly what they chose to do.

Why not, instead, plant the entire real estate of the book with the stories that the women themselves choose to tell about what they did, why they did it, and how they did it? Then, let the readers compare this fresh new information with the dominant and overwhelmingly persistent ink, news, and reports already out there, describing how men did it or how "only" a few women do it.

Give the entire space over to the stories about the women and then let the readers conclude for themselves the differences these women bring to their positions of leadership or executive roles. Allow the reader to experience the lives of these women as they grew up over time and made their career decisions. Allow the readers to compare or contrast what they see in this description of the marketplace from the perspectives of the women interviewed. Let the reader decide.

Writing about exemplary women in leadership from this perspective would be like what Fran Whitteley once said: "Ginger Rogers did every step as Fred Astaire [did], only backwards and in heels."

Lesson: Frankly, I think it would be interesting to hear a little more from Ginger.

TWO GOOD WOMEN

The *Los Angeles Times*' obituary section on February 8, 2008, included commemoratives of two dramatically different women, but leaders both.[1]

Adrienne A. Hall (1926–2008) was an "[a]d executive [who] broke barriers for women," while Ruth Stafford Peale (1906–2008) was the "[p]astor's wife [who] co-founded Guideposts." Twenty years apart in age, they represented a gaping spectrum between women who made the world different by their accomplishments. One was a path-breaking female business entrepreneur; the other was an enduring aide to her husband's mission. I would not want to participate in a world today that had not benefited from their individual contributions.

Ms. Hall founded her own advertising firm (Hall & Levine Advertising, formed with Joan Levine) long before it was the acceptable thing for women to do. She made a better success of her firm in 1970 than most women do thirty-plus years later. With clients that included Max Factor and Neutrogena, her agency received the Advertising Award of the Year in 1976 from the Western States Advertising Agency Association. In 1980, her firm was acquired by Foote, Cone & Belding.

She and some friends founded the Committee of 200 in 1982, one of the very first women-mentoring-women in leadership groups. Later, she was active in the International Women's Forum, which grew from 1,000 members in 1985 to over 4,800 women of note in sixty-one affiliates in forty-two countries today.

The second obituary on the same date was for Ruth Stafford Peale, who co-founded with her husband Guideposts (1945), the "global inspirational organization led by Norman Vincent Peale."[2] She was a religious leader in her own right but handled publication of all of his sermons for the Peale Center for Christian Living in Pawling, New York.

More importantly, she encouraged him to persist in the face of countless rejections from publishers. When he was discouraged enough to toss a draft of *The Power of Positive Thinking* into the trash in frustration, she took it back and persuaded him to continue. Eventually, the book sold over twenty-one million copies.

One woman was an innovator on the outside, the other on the inside of a family, and both changed the world and our lives. They were from opposite poles of the political spectrum, yet in all likelihood, each would probably have respected the other woman and her accomplishments. They both certainly would have been civil to each other—lessons we all could take from their exemplary lives, among many other stories.

But thirty years have passed, and we take their revolutionary contributions for granted today, in our world more obsessed with *Sex and the City*, *Desperate Housewives*, *Cashmere Mafia*, *Lipstick Jungle*, and other Stiletto Spin-Sister Stereotypes.

Lesson: These good women and a whole host of others laid the groundwork for this generation to choose what they want to do and what they want to become as women. Today's generation received the gift of choice by women either at the end of, or in between, the spectrum represented by Ms. Hall and Ms. Peale. Let's hope the stories about today's young women are equally inspiring.

THE TYPE E* WOMAN

Dr. Harriet B. Braiker (1948–2004) wrote the book *The Type E* Woman: How to Overcome the Stress of Being *Everything to Everybody*.[3] Her most impressive message was that "[s]triving for excellence motivates you; striving for perfection is demoralizing."

Two other insightful books by Dr. Braiker include *The Disease to Please: Curing the People-Pleasing Syndrome* (McGraw-Hill: 2000), and *Who's Pulling Your Strings? How to Break the Cycle of Manipulation and Regain Control of Your Life* (McGraw-Hill: 2003). As the titles clearly indicate, Dr. Braiker's writings were focused on teaching women how to stop being manipulated by others.

Harriet Beryl Braiker was born in Los Angeles. She graduated summa cum laude from the University of California, Los Angeles (UCLA), where she was elected to Phi Beta Kappa and won a National Science Foundation research scholarship. In 1975, she received a doctorate in clinical and social psychology from UCLA.[4]

She began her career at the RAND Corporation analyzing health policies, including alcohol abuse and prison incarceration, for the federal government. In 1982, she was a consultant to the National Institute of Alcohol Abuse and Alcoholism, a research project on women and alcoholism from which she developed many of the insights in her books. She established her private psychotherapy and management consulting practice in 1986, and wrote and spoke extensively on the subject of stress and women's issues.

She was a senior vice president of Lexicon Communications, a Pasadena-based crisis management training and consulting firm founded with her husband, Steven B. Fink.

Her writings tapped an extensive body of research drawn from a nation-wide survey of 1,000 working women conducted by the Gallup Organization (1987–1989). They discovered that many high-achieving women were experiencing stress while trying to excel in both personal life and career. Dr. Braiker observed that their "everything to everyone" behavior was consistent with the Type A syndrome among men.

Her writing and consulting helped women identify their Type E behavior through a self-test then deal with the symptoms, first by assessing whether they sustained false premises that led to the behavior and, second, by developing alternative strategies or coping tactics to reduce stress and enhance personal resistance to stress.

"The Type E woman needs to redefine the set of behaviors that she *herself* must actually do in order to satisfy her own standards for fulfillment and excellence in her various roles."[5]

She said women need to recognize that stressful reactions were internal, over which women needed to exert control. "They must learn active fight-back strategies as a way to gain control over the external demands and internal beliefs, expectations, conflicts, and pressures that comprise the Type E ["everything to everyone"] dilemma."[6]

Her ten-step exercise for learning better coping strategies included these:[7]

1. Redefine role requirements.

2. Rank-order re-prioritized activities.

3. Create and rehearse "No" scripts.

4. Schedule pleasurable activities.

5. Establish brainstorming and problem-solving sessions.

6. Use guided imagery and relaxation to desensitize stress.

7. Use role-playing and script-rehearsals to inoculate against stress.

8. Learn to "talk yourself down."

9. Take mini-vacations.

10. Use time-management analysis to improve efficiencies.

She used these exercises to build a twenty-one-day Mental Workout Training Program to "break out of self-destructive behaviors" and move forward toward greater personal happiness and success.

Lesson: Personal happiness and success are matters of choice and learning.

"JUST" 43 YEARS AGO

We often read that there are "just" seventeen or twenty percent of the top public company board seats occupied by women, but we forget that we have a choice as to whether we want to look at those who made it to the top or whether we want to focus on those who did not. Imagine what it must have been like to be the truly first, solo, lone woman to be appointed to a major U.S. corporate board of directors—"just" 43 years ago.

She was Patricia Roberts Harris (1924–1985), appointed to the IBM corporate board in 1971. She was a "two-fer": a woman and a woman of color. She was awesome: lawyer, African American, ambassador to Luxembourg, U.S. secretary of three cabinet level departments (HUD, HEW, HHS), and law school dean at Howard University. The reality is that Ms. Harris was "first" wherever she aspired to succeed.

Every year since 1971, the total number of women in Fortune 500 boards across the nation has increased by an average of twenty women, and the number for Fortune 501–1000 firms has increased by almost ten women. This means the actual number of women *added* was probably even higher, because, of course, some women retired or resigned in those years.

What was happening in 1971? Forty-three years ago, the *New York Times* published the *Pentagon Papers*. Richard Nixon put a freeze on wages, prices, and rent. China entered the UN General Assembly, and Taiwan left. Intel announced the first microprocessor, the Intel 4004. Barack Obama was ten years old. Hillary Clinton was twenty-four years old, and John McCain was thirty-five years old and in his fourth of five and a half years as a POW in Vietnam.

In 2012, Virginia Rometty became the first female president and CEO to take charge at IBM. In 2014, Mary Barra became the first female CEO of a major U.S. auto manufacturer, General Motors. By 2014, there were twenty-four women CEOs of Fortune 500 firms and another twenty-seven women CEOs of companies at the next tier, Fortune 500–1000.[8]

In the span of one career (forty-three years), women have advanced to leadership in significant numbers in U.S. business. The focus should remain on their achievements. Any other focus takes away from their accomplishments.

Lesson: Leadership begins with a first, but progress is measured by all those who learn from that inspiration.

FIRST WOMEN CORPORATE DIRECTORS

While Patricia Roberts Harris is recognized as the first woman (in the modern era) to be named to a public company board of directors (IBM,

1971), there have been two other, earlier outstanding women directors who rose to their positions by more traditional means.[9]

Lettie Pate Whitehead Evans (1872–1953)

Lettie Pate Whitehead Evans served as chairwoman of the board of the Whitehead Holding Co., as well as head of other financial interests. She was a savvy business woman in the soft drink industry and was the first woman to serve as a director of a major American corporation when she was appointed in 1934 to the board of Coca-Cola Co., where she served until 1953.[10]

She married Joseph Brown Whitehead, an attorney, in 1895. Whitehead was instrumental in gaining exclusive rights to bottle Coca-Cola nationwide. When he died in 1906, she took over the family business (the Whitehead Holding Company) and real estate interests (the Whitehead Realty Company).

Coca-Cola confirmed that she served on its board from 1934 to 1953, but her information has yet to be included on the "History" portion of their website.

Ms. Evans established a scholarship grant program through the Lettie Pace Whitehead Foundation[11] and the Lettie Pace Evans Foundation[12] to support charitable organizations.

Marjorie Merriweather Post (1887–1973)

Marjorie Merriweather Post inherited family wealth and the Postum Cereal Company from her father, Charles William Post, the inventor of Postum (the coffee substitute), Post Toasties, and Grape-Nuts.[13]

As she was an only child, her father taught her everything about his business. When he died in 1914, she inherited everything and became the company president. She married E. F. Hutton, the Wall Street broker/financier, in 1920. They transformed Postum Cereal Company Ltd. through aggressive acquisitions and took the company public in 1922. Hutton took over as president in 1923. The company became the General Foods Corporation in 1929.

In 1935, Marjorie Post divorced Hutton and married Joseph E. Davies, the American ambassador to the Soviet Union. In 1936, she became a director of the General Foods Corporation.

During their marriage and travels to Russia, she collected extensive works of art that later would be housed in Hillwood Estate Museum &

Gardens,[14] established in 1955, as the premier collection of Russian imperial art outside of Russia.

They divorced in 1955, and in 1958, she married Herbert A. May, Jr., heir to the May department stores.

The Kraft Foods Corporation website has no mention of Marjorie Post or of her outstanding role in its history.

Lesson: We could do a better job of memorializing the unique contributions of women in business and finance. We could learn a great deal more from our early women in leadership.

Barbara Alice Ringer

We should not forget the contributions of great women like Barbara Alice Ringer (1925–2009), who spent twenty-one years crafting the new terms and conditions of copyright protections and then educated and lobbied Congress until it was finally enacted as the Copyright Act of 1976.[15]

Born in Lafayette, Indiana, Ms. Ringer was a Phi Beta Kappa graduate of George Washington University (1945), received a masters of arts degree from the same university (1947), and graduated from Columbia Law School (1949) in the post-war economy, when very few women pursued advanced degrees. She lived her later years, after retiring from the Library of Congress, in Lexington, Virginia.[16]

In 2013, the U.S. Copyright Office established the Barbara A. Ringer Copyright Honors Program ("Ringer Honors Program"), which offers eighteen to twenty-four month paid fellowships for attorneys ("Ringer Fellows") in the initial stages of their careers who demonstrate exceptional ability and interest in copyright law.[17]

Lesson: There is a certain irony in the realization that something as pervasive in our economy as the protections of copyright law would have been crafted by such an unsung woman in leadership.

Margaret Lena Walker

Another great lady of business, Margaret ("Maggie") Lena Walker (1867–1934), was the first female banker.[18]

In 1899, she was elected the right worthy grand secretary of the Independent Order of St. Luke, the highest-ranking position in the organization. She later became secretary-treasurer, a position she held until 1934. The Independent Order of St. Luke was a fraternal burial society (comparable to a mutual benefit organization) established in 1867 in Baltimore,

Maryland. The society administered to the sick and the aged, promoted humanitarian causes, and encouraged individual self-help and integrity.

In 1902, Maggie Walker founded a newspaper, the *St. Luke Herald*, to communicate and advocate at the local level. In 1903, she chartered the St. Luke Penny Savings Bank, which was a precursor to the micro-lending organizations developed later by Mohammed Yunus (the Grameen Bank and South Bank, Chicago). Ms. Walker earned the recognition of being the first woman to charter a bank in the United States. She remained on the board of directors as chair after the bank merged with two other Richmond banks to become the Consolidated Bank and Trust Company, which thrived until 2010 as the oldest continually African American–operated bank in the country. At that time, it was merged into Premier Bank.[19]

In addition, about 1905, Ms. Walker established the St. Luke Emporium as a retail millinery store. Such outlets provided work to the community and an outlet for resale or modification of women, children, and men's clothing.

Lesson: There is something special about women who succeed in multiple endeavors. They are multifaceted mentors.

Muriel Siebert

Muriel "Mickie" Siebert (1928–2013) is considered "the grande dame of American finance."[20] She was the founder and president of Muriel Siebert & Co., Inc. a New York Stock Exchange (NYSE) brokerage firm she established in 1967. It is the only woman-owned firm with a national footprint, including seven branches and a municipal affiliate (Siebert Brandford Shank & Co. LLC—rated among the top public finance firms in the United States).

Ms. Siebert became the first woman member of the NYSE after many battles with the male financial community. She served a five-year term (1977–1982) as the superintendent of the New York State Banking Department under Governor Hugh Carey. In 1996, Muriel Siebert Capital Markets Group Inc. did a reverse-merger with J. Michaels Inc., a New York retail furniture corporation, with Siebert Financial Corp. being the surviving public firm holding shares on NASDAQ. According to the 2010 Proxy Filing, Siebert Financial Corp. had six directors, four of whom were women.[21]

In 1999, while president of the New York Women's Agenda, a coalition of more than 100 women's organizations, Ms. Siebert developed a personal finance program to improve the financial literacy of our nation's young people.

The program was initially designed to teach two essential financial management skills—managing a checkbook and understanding the use and abuse of credit cards. It has been expanded to include topics such as the basics of money, banking, credit, budgeting, taxes, insurance, and investing.

Ms. Siebert attended, but did not complete, college at what is now Case Western Reserve University, was awarded eighteen honorary doctoral degrees, and was inducted into several halls of fame.

She was one of four women of Wall Street who were the focus of the 2003 film, *Risk/Reward* directed by Elizabeth Holder and Xan Parker and executive producer Peter Gilbert.[22] The film (now on DVD) highlighted the challenges met and mastered by outstanding women in finance.

In late March 2008, Muriel Siebert was interviewed by Rehema Ellis for the "Making a Difference" segment on *NBC Nightly News* with Brian Williams, where she described the origins and her reasons for establishing her Personal Financial Program, initially piloted in the New York School System with the New York City Department of Education and now serving over 280 schools in ten states.[23]

In March 2009, Muriel Siebert was inducted into the Junior Achievement's U.S. Business Hall of Fame.

Lesson: How many different ways are there to learn how a woman of achievement built her career? Articles, books, interviews, movies and videos, websites of the businesses that the women created, the programs they instituted, and the proxy statements that describe their business decisions over the decades? Is this not mentoring?

Dr. Elinor Ostrom

Elinor Ostrom (1933–2012) was the first woman to receive the Nobel Prize in Economic Sciences (2009) since the prize was established in 1969. Until her death in 2012 in Bloomington, Illinois, she was the Arthur F. Bentley Professor of Political Science in the College of Arts and Sciences and a professor in the School of Public and Environmental Affairs at Indiana University-Bloomington. Indiana University was rightfully proud.[24] She received her bachelor's, master's, and doctoral degrees from the University of California at Los Angeles (UCLA).

She and her co-prize-winner, Oliver E. Williamson of the University of California, Berkeley, were recognized for their work in the field of "economic governance: the organization of cooperation."

Her work related in particular to the challenges of "Tragedy of Freedom in a Commons," a subject initially discussed by William Forster Lloyd, a political economist at Oxford University, in 1832. Economic issues surrounding shared resources (common pastureland or fishing grounds, for example) generated vigorous debate as to how best to manage those scarce resources. A key question was whether government should dictate the allocation of resources or if vested interests could self-regulate resources more effectively.

The Nobel Committee's announcement described Dr. Ostrom's major contribution to economic thought:

> *[She] has challenged the conventional wisdom that common property is poorly managed and should be either regulated by central authorities or privatized. Based on numerous studies of user-managed fish stocks, pastures, woods, lakes, and groundwater basins, Ostrom concludes that the outcomes are, more often than not, better than predicted by standard theories. She observes that resource users frequently develop sophisticated mechanisms for decision-making and rule enforcement to handle conflicts of interest, and she characterizes the rules that promote successful outcomes.*[25]

Dr. Ostrom had published articles, reviews, and books since 1965.[26] Two books are worth recommending from her impressive collaborations:

Understanding Institutional Diversity:[27] "What emerges from Elinor Ostrom's book is precisely what the title suggests—an understanding of the diverse nature of institutions that exist in human societies to promote human cooperation or to hinder it."[28]

Governing the Commons:[29] "In this ambitious, provocative, and very useful book Ostrom combines a lucid theoretical framework with a series of diverse and richly detailed case studies . . . she tightly reviews and critiques extant models of cooperation and collective action and argues powerfully that communities of actors are sometimes able to maintain a common resource for long periods of time without outside intervention."[30]

Lesson: Ultimately, the world will recognize and shine a bright light on well-reasoned alternative perspectives and independent thought. Ultimately, women will learn that economics is a tool appropriate to fostering shared community and cooperative goals.

EIGHT

Conclusion

These are the collected stories of many mentees observing mentors and tapping the wealth of knowledge and insight they possess—often without the mentors ever knowing that that learning and growth had occurred. Outstanding women taught the younger women something that lasted a lifetime. They inspired the younger women by their writing, by their exemplary efforts, by their work, or by their achievements. Men, too, including brothers and fathers, taught the young women the lessons they wished to convey—lessons that would serve them well in the challenging global marketplace.

Mentorship is all about "whom do you admire" and why. We do not choose who our family members, our teachers, or most of the people whose lives intersect with ours are. But we can either ignore the contributions they have to offer to our lives—whether positive or negative—or we can tap the wisdom that surrounds us. What might these individuals teach us as we grow and mature? And why would mentorship in our careers, as adults, be any different from assimilating the lessons from family, friends, and teachers?

Therefore, it is more about our capacity to listen and learn as a protégé than it is about the mentors who might surround us in our lives. The challenge is to be a great student of life and lessons, rather than wait for some perfect one-on-one relationship within a highly structured corporate program.

These stories, like the tale of Telemachus, provide us with an abundant resource of wisdom about true mentorship. What are the most important of those lessons?

THE LESSONS OF MENTOR

#1 There is an essential human desire to search for someone else to solve our problems.

The Odyssey is an epic story of *deus ex machina*, the involvement of the gods in the lives of humans. Telemachus and Odysseus both prayed to the gods for solutions. But the gods were not the ones who took action against the challenges faced by the father and son.

#2 We often have to reach that certain point of absolute frustration with the way things are, now, before we will undertake change.

Mentor told the suitors to leave and was ridiculed. Athena told Telemachus to kick them out, but he collapsed in tears, unprepared and not yet mature enough to benefit from her wisdom.

#3 Sometimes the solution is not to face the challenge immediately and directly but, rather, to go seek more information, more personal development, more resolve, and more resources.

Telemachus took the initiative to get out of his situation and pursue answers from friends of his father from the great wars. If his father were alive, that would imply one set of options; if he were not alive, the son would have to construct options of his own. Telemachus took the initiative by preparing for the journey and the search.

#4 Real growth occurs during the search, not by actions of the mentor.

During his journey in search of his father, Telemachus had to take charge of the ship and its crew. He had to talk with the great leaders who had battled at Troy. He learned he would be dealt with as the adult he had become.

#5 At some point, the most important decision is to return home, take on the challenges, trust yourself and your actions, and be ready to deal with the consequences.

Unlike all of the challenges that Odysseus faced, nothing substantive happened during Telemachus's journey except for the decision to return home and take ownership of that to which he was entitled.

#6 Mentors and mentees strategize to overcome their shared obstacles: each has a value to offer the other.

Telemachus had a small, specific, and key role to play in eliminating the weaponry of the suitors—a role appropriate to his skills and crucial to the success of the plan. After the suitors were slaughtered,

Telemachus showed his new maturity and initiative when he persuaded his father to pardon the few innocents.

Mentorship, therefore, is the story of growth from potential into mature talent. It is not a story of being helped, trained, coached, protected, or guided by some mysterious hand. It is the tale of decision-making in the face of adversity, the value of separating one's own self from the fray in order to gain perspective and to satisfy a hunger and thirst for knowledge and information with which one can address and slay apparently superior challenges.

THE MODERN MENTOR AND PROTÉGÉ RELATIONSHIP

A mentor is a seasoned professional, an accomplished amateur, or someone who is a leader in his/her field. In the epic story of *The Odyssey*, Athena was the goddess of skill and intelligence, much as an artisan is someone capable of training both journeyman and apprentice.

Today, corporations are expected to create "mentor programs" in which senior employees work with junior employees to teach them the ins and outs of the business, as they know it. Executive coaches advise women entrepreneurs to search for mentors among business organizations or small business development advisors to learn at the hand of someone with whom they establish some vague relationship. To search for a mentor is to search for skills and intelligence that one does not yet have, but which one wishes to have.

Too often, the mentor-protégé relationship, especially for women, has been re-defined as an interpersonal relationship: a plea for some *deus ex machina*. Women often expect there will be a hyper-dependent relationship where the key considerations are these: What can the protégé get from the mentor? What can she "take away" from the relationship? Who is the perfect wise woman-seer-crone who could give the protégé just what she needs?

This artificial mentor relationship sometimes looks like an extension of "helicopter parenting" into the corporate marketplace. Are mentees expecting to be handed the answers to all their challenges? How much knowledge can mentors spoon-feed today's workers? Who has to do the growing and the hard work of learning? Do executives have any available time to perform the training tasks that mentees expect in today's marketplace?

For women, mentoring might be perceived as a situation where each party is expected to give up more than she gets. This could produce either weakness or sacrifice. The junior woman in the workplace wants help. She may be uncertain of herself or her talent; she may even doubt herself or be unwilling or unable to develop her talents through her own initiative. Why, then, would a senior woman find any benefit or value from devoting attention to such an employee?

The senior woman also might be searching for help. Some say that women at the top of the corporate ladder today do not mentor up-and-coming younger women because they have their hands full trying to protect themselves from the sabotage of men *and* other women in the organization. Some women at the top mentor only women outside of their professional circle and only those who are significantly worse off than they are: abused women, battered women, women of the street, and other women deserving great pity. By helping only women at the very bottom of the pecking order, women at the top are assured of finding grateful recipients of their largess and never have to face "sabotage savvy" women or the "Power Dead-Even Rule" of jealous wannabes.

In both of these cases, junior and senior women are running on empty. Mentoring ends up just not being worth the effort on a level comparable to the ways it works best for men in corporate life. Perhaps another view of the modern mentor relationship would be appropriate for women.

A mentee is a protégé—someone with talent worthy of further development. Not everyone can be guided by a mentor—only individuals with some inherent initiative or willingness to take on challenges will be worthy of mentoring. Real protégés are those who possess special talent— unique and valued skills that if honed properly, might actually improve the quality of the profession or the art. Protégés respect and admire the mentor as someone who is wiser and more knowledgeable—someone whom they would like to emulate.

The goal of a mentor-protégé relationship is that each party be prepared to perform her appropriate role in the face of shared challenges. The mentor does not teach the protégé directly but, rather, pushes the protégé out into a sea of learning experiences in order to grow. If the protégé matures in the process, she returns from that experience possessing even greater judgment and value.

With typical mentoring relationships between junior and senior men in the workplace, we seldom encounter a one-way relationship. Rather, it is a mutually beneficial deal: each party perceives that he will get more in return than what each invests in the other. In a guy-to-guy mentor relationship, the senior one believes he will benefit by working and an up-and-coming superstar who is dynamic, creative, hard-hitting, gung-ho, and who can add pizzazz to the senior's already bright aura. The junior one, for his part, believes he will benefit by his association with the experienced, weathered senior by bringing new insight and perspective to the valued, seasoned mentor.

To create positive mentor-mentee outcomes is to focus less on the relationship and more on the performance. It is the mentee who must do the heavy lifting—learn and grow, primarily through observation and emulation. Mentoring is about power: dominant and subordinate, in fact. Mentoring is a temporary superior-to-subordinate relationship, which, if it is successful, disappears to the benefit and advancement of both participants.

Imagine, if you could, a different tale of *The Odyssey* where Athena had allowed Telemachus to stay at home, and she alone tried to "help" him face his demons. What if Telemachus had never gone to sea, traveled the world by himself, or spoken with the wise individuals whom he encountered during his journey? When the real challenge came, after his father returned home, would Telemachus have been able to take on his share of the tasks required to defeat the suitors? Another entirely different story would then have unfolded.

The same is true of the individuals in these stories. They tapped the wisdom that surrounded them more than they were taught explicitly the lessons of each encounter. They took purpose and insight from the role models and incorporated those experiences into their own lives and careers. Some of the best lessons came from unintentional example-setting. Some of the best learning experiences came from the interpretation applied by the mind of the mentee rather than the explicit teachings of the mentor. Some examples came from the writing of the mentor, from writings about the mentor, or from mentors whom the mentee never met in person. A mentor does not have to be present to teach a protégé the lessons she/he must learn.

The reality of modern life is that the one who seeks to grow is also the one who must do the search and the learning. The wisdom surrounds you. It is up to you to identify the talent you believe is worthwhile, the lessons you wish to incorporate, and the role models whom you would like to emulate in your own manner, fashion, and style. The wisdom of mentors is everywhere—in your memories, the stories you tell yourself and each other, the pages you read, and the people you meet. How you tap that wisdom and make it your very own is the gift of mentorship.

Notes

CHAPTER TWO: AT SCHOOL

1. Elizabeth Ghaffari. *Outstanding in Their Field: How Women Corporate Directors Succeed* (Santa Barbara, CA: Praeger, 2008), 81.

2. Christine Todd Whitman. *It's My Party Too: The Battle for the Heart of the GOP and the Future of America* (New York, NY: The Penguin Press HC, January 31, 2005), 56–57.

3. Lotte Bailyn. "Academic Careers and Gender Equity: Lessons Learned from MIT." *Gender, Work and Organization.* Vol. 10, no. 2 (March 2003), 138 http://www.nuigalway.ie/equality/documents/gwo_paper_about_mit.pdf

4. Bailyn, 137–153.

5. Bailyn, 140.

6. Bailyn, 139.

7. Bailyn, 142.

8. Bailyn, 141.

9. Virginia Valian. *Why So Slow? The Advancement of Women* (Cambridge, MA: MIT Press, 1998)

10. Bailyn, 142.

11. Valian, 2.

12. Malcolm Gladwell. *Blink: The Power of Thinking without Thinking* (New York, NY: Little Brown & Company, 2005), 249–250.

13. Lotte Bailyn. *Gender Equity in Academia: Lessons from the MIT Experience*, Occasional Paper 2 (Cambridge, MA: The Athena Project, no date), 9.

14. Bailyn, 147–149.

CHAPTER THREE: AT PLAY

1. George Santana. *Life of Reason, Reason in Common Sense* (New York, NY: Charles Scribner's Sons, 1905), 284.

2. "Title IX's Next Hurdle: Three Decades after Its Passage, Rule That Leveled Field for Girls Faces Test from Administration," *Wall Street Journal*, Business Section (July 6, 2005). http://online.wsj.com/news/articles /SB112061338370378102 (accessed 2/26/2014).

3. Karen Blumenthal. *Let Me Play The Story of Title IX; The Law That Changed the Future of Girls in America* (New York, NY: Atheneum Books for Young Readers, July 1, 2005).

4. Rudyard Kipling. "If," *Poems & Poets*. Poetry Foundation. http://www .poetryfoundation.org/poem/175772 (accessed 2/26/2014).

5. World Tennis Association. "About the WTA" http://www.wtatennis.com /scontent/article/2951989/title/about-the-wta (accessed 2/26/2014).

6. Billie Jean King. *Pressure Is a Privilege: Lessons I've Learned from Life and the Battle of the Sexes* (New York, NY: LifeTime Media Inc., August 12, 2008).

7. Kathrine Switzer. *Marathon Woman: Running the Race to Revolutionize Women's Sports* (Cambridge, MA: Da Capo Press, March 30, 2007). http:// kathrineswitzer.com/ (accessed 2/26/2014).

8. LA Leggers® is a registered trademark of The LA Leggers Inc.

9. Carol Hymowitz. "All Companies Need Innovation; Hasbro Finds a New Magic," *The Wall Street Journal* (February 26, 2007), B1. http://online.wsj .com/news/articles/SB117244992317418824 (accessed 2/26/2014).

10. Felice N. Schwartz. "Management Women and the New Facts of Life," *Harvard Business Review* Reprint #89110 (Cambridge, MA, January 1, 1989).

11. Tamar Lewin. "'Mommy Career Track' Sets Off a Furor," *New York Times*. (March 8, 1989). http://www.nytimes.com/1989/03/08/us/mommy-career-track-sets-off-a-furor.html (accessed 2/26/2014).

12. Theodore Lauppert. "Lemonade Stand." http://theodor.lauppert.ws/games /lemonade.htm (accessed 2/26/2014) and http://www.ae4rv.com/games /lemonade.htm (accessed 2/26/2014). *Lemonade Stand* was a game, written in the BASIC programming language, designed by Bob Jamison of the Minnesota Educational Computing Consortium (MECC) in 1973. Charlie Kellner, founder of the Apple Education Dept., migrated the game to the Apple II platform in February of 1979. Today *Lemonade Stand* is a $10 downloadable software program for the PC.

13. Pat Heim, PhD, and Susan Murphy, PhD with Susan Golant. *In the Company of Women: Indirect Aggression Among Women: Why We Hurt Each Other and How to Stop* (New York, NY: Jeremy Tarcher, May 26, 2003), 49 ff.

14. Pauline R. Clance and Suzanne A. Imes. "The Imposter Phenomenon in High Achieving Women: Dynamics and Therapeutic Intervention," *Psychotherapy: Theory, Research & Practice*, 15 no. 3 (1978), 241–247.

15. "Michelle Obama, Sonia Sotomayor and the Imposter Syndrome." Video and transcript from *The Rachel Maddow Show* (June 4, 2009), *Women and Talent* blog. http://womenandtalent.com/84/michelle-obama-sonia-sotomayor-and-the-impostor-syndrome/ (accessed 2/26/2014).

CHAPTER FOUR: AT WORK

1. Alvin Toffler. *Future Shock* (New York, NY: Random House, 1970).

2. Richard Deitsch. "Performance with a Purpose," *The Costco Connection* (June 2008), 20 ff. Courtesy of *The Costco Connection.* http://www.costcoconnection.com/connection/200806/?u1=texterity#pg22 (accessed 2/26/2014).

3. Independent Means Inc. website: http://www.independentmeans.com/imi/index.php (accessed 2/26/2014).

4. Linda A. Hill, Melinda B. Conrad, and Nancy Kamprath. *Joline Godfrey and the Polaroid Corp. (A) and (B)* Harvard Business School Prod. #492037-PDF-ENG (A) and #492038-PDF-ENG (B) (Cambridge, MA: March 18, 1992).

5. Joline Godfrey. *No More Frogs to Kiss, 99 Ways to Give Economic Power to Girls* (New York, NY: HarperCollins: 1995).

6. Amazon.com book description of *No More Frogs to Kiss.* http://www.amazon.com/No-More-Frogs-Kiss-Economic/dp/0887306594 (accessed 2/26/2014).

7. Gloria Steinem. Foreword to *No More Frogs to Kiss*, xvii and x.

8. Joline Godfrey. *Our Wildest Dreams: Women Making Money, Having Fun, Doing Good* (New York, NY; Harper Perennial: 1993).

9. Joline Godfrey. *Twenty $ecrets to Money and Independence: The DollarDiva's Guide to Life* (New York, NY: St. Martin's Press: 2000).

10. Joline Godfrey. *Golden Guides from St. Martin's Press*; 1st edition (January 15, 2000) (Berkeley, CA: Ten Speed Press: 2003).

11. "University of Maine Foundation to Honor Five Alumni at 75th Anniversary Celebration," University of Maine Foundation http://www.umainefoundation.org/news/news43.html (accessed 2/26/2014).

12. Linda A. Hill. "Joline Godfrey and the Polaroid Corp. (B)." Harvard Business School Supplement 492-038, March 1992 (Revised March 1995). http://hbr.org/search/492038 (accessed 2/26/2014).

13. Joline Godfrey. "The Case against Economic Development for Women," *Community Investments* 10 no. 2 (Federal Reserve Bank of San Francisco: Spring, 1998), 1. http://www.frbsf.org/community-development/files/Godfrey_The_Case_against_Economic_Development_for_Women.pdf (accessed 2/26/2014).

14. Amy Boaz. Review of *Written by Herself* in *Library Journal.* (1992). http://www.amazon.com/Written-Herself-Autobiographies-American-Anthology/dp/0679736336 (accessed 2/26/2014).

15. Jill Ker Conway. *The Road from Coorain* (New York, NY: Knopf, 1989); PBS Masterpiece Theatre movie by the same name was released December 14, 2003. http://www.pbs.org/wgbh/masterpiece/coorain/ (accessed 2/26/2014).

16. "President Jill Ker Conway," Smithipedia. http://sophia.smith.edu/blog/smithipedia/administration/president-jill-ker-conway/ (accessed 2/26/2014).

17. "Nike Helps Establish Jill Ker Conway Fellowship Fund in MIT Political Science Department." Press Release, Nike Inc. (February 23, 2012). http://nikeinc.com/news/nike-helps-establish-jill-ker-conway-fellowship-fund-in-mit-political-science-department (accessed 2/26/2014).

18. Max Nisen. "How Nike Solved Its Sweatshop Problem," *Business Insider.* (May 9, 2013). http://www.businessinsider.com/how-nike-solved-its-sweatshop-problem-2013-5 (accessed 2/26/2014)

Nike Proxy Statement, August 10, 2001. http://www.sec.gov/Archives/edgar/data/320187/000109581101503848/v74222ddef14a.txt (accessed 2/26/2014).

19. "Chairman Jill Conway Steps Down." Press Release, Lend Lease Corporation (May 29, 2003). http://phx.corporate-ir.net/phoenix.zhtml?c=186950&p=irol-newsArticle&ID=1599501 (accessed 2/26/2014).

20. Jill Ker Conway, editor. *Written by Herself: Autobiographies of American Women: An Anthology* (New York, NY: Vintage Books, 1992) and *Written by Herself: Volume 2: Women's Memoirs From Britain, Africa, Asia and the United States* (New York, NY: Vintage Books, 1996).

21. Jill Ker Conway, *The Road from Coorain* (New York, NY; Knopf, 1989).

22. "President Obama Awards 2012 National Humanities Medals." Press Release, National Endowment for the Humanities (July 10, 2013). http://www.neh.gov/news/press-release/2013-07-08 (accessed 2/26/2014).

23. Patrick Moran. "Jill Ker Conway and James Crawford Receive the AC." *Who's Who News* (June 11, 2013). http://www.connectweb.com.au/news/whos-who/jill-ker-conway-and-james-crawford-awarded-the-ac.aspx (accessed 2/26/2014).

24. Gary Strauss. "'Queen of the Corporate Jungle' Stalks Annual Meetings," *USA Today.* (April 27, 2003). http://usatoday30.usatoday.com/money/companies/management/2003-04-27-shareholders-davis_x.htm (accessed 2/26/2014).

25. Richard Jerome. "Evelyn Y. Davis," *People Magazine Archive* 45 no. 20 (May 20, 1996). http://www.people.com/people/archive/article/0,,20141327,00.html (accessed 2/26/2014).

26. Robert Trigaux. "Executives Cower from This Gadfly in the Ointment," *St. Petersburg Times.* (May 22, 2002). http://www.sptimes.com/2002/05/22/Columns/Executives_cower_from.shtml (accessed 2/26/2014).

Samantha Bomkamp, Associated Press. "Blankfein, Dimon, and Almost Every Other CEO in America Knows Evelyn Davis," *BusinessInsider.* (July 13, 2012). http://www.businessinsider.com/evelyn-davis-shareholder-advocate-2012-7 (accessed 2/26/2014).

27. Christina Rexrode, Associated Press. "The Loudest Shareholder Activist Ready for a Break," *USA Today.* (July 13, 2012). http://usatoday30.usatoday.com

/money/media/story/2012-07-13/evelyn-y-davis-gadfly-retires/56203956/1 (accessed 2/26/2014).

28. "Evelyn Davis: Editor, Highlights and Lowlights." http://www.sec.gov /spotlight/proxyprocess/bio052507/eydavis.pdf (accessed 2/26/2014).

29. "Evelyn Y. Davis Gives $100,000 to Penn for Scholarship," *Penn News.* (January 16, 2004). http://www.upenn.edu/pennnews/news/evelyn-y-davis-gives-100000-penn-scholarship (accessed 2/26/2014).

30. "Mrs. Evelyn Y. Davis and the Evelyn Y. Davis Foundation Make Charitable Contribution to National Trust for Historic Preservation, as Announced by Richard Moe, President of the National Trust," *PRNEWSWIRE* Press Release. (May 11, 2005).   http://www.prnewswire.com/news-releases/mrs-evelyn-y-davis-and-the-evelyn-y-davis-foundation-make-charitable-contribution-to-national-trust-for-historic-preservation-as-announced-by-richard-moe-president-of-the-national-trust-54371322.html (accessed 2/26/2014).

31. "Evelyn Y. Davis Creates Undergraduate Scholarships," *UNC School of Journalism and Mass Communication* (August 20, 2009). http://www.jomc.unc .edu/News-Items/Evelyn-Y-Davis-creates-undergraduate-scholarships (accessed 2/26/2014).

32. "Shareholder Activist Evelyn Davis Creates Fund at Yale Center for Corporate Governance," *Yale News.* (November 6, 2007). http://news.yale.edu/2007/11/06/ shareholder-activist-evelyn-davis-creates-fund-yale-center-corporate-governance (accessed 2/26/2014).

33. Carol S. Wood. "Evelyn Y. Davis, Shareholder Advocate, Makes Generous Gift to Support Programs at U.Va," *UVA Today.* (January 8, 2008). http://news .virginia.edu/content/evelyn-y-davis-shareholder-advocate-makes-generous-gift-support-programs-uva (accessed 2/26/2014).

34. "Evelyn Y. Davis, Shareholder Advocate, and the Evelyn Y. Davis Foundation Donate $100,000 to Riggs Emergency Department at Baylor University Medical Center at Dallas," *Baylor Health Care Online Newsroom.* (December 8, 2008). http://media.baylorhealth.com/releases/Evelyn-Y-Davis-Shareholder-Advocate-and-the-Evelyn-Y-Davis-Foundation-Donate-100-000-to-Riggs-Emergency-Department-at-Baylor-University-Medical-Center-at-Dallas (accessed 2/26/2014).

35. "Evelyn Y. Davis Donates $1 Million to the George Washington University," Press Release of the George Washington University. (December 25, 2012). http:// mediarelations.gwu.edu/evelyn-y-davis-donates-1-million-george-washington-university (accessed 2/26/2014).

36. "Evelyn Y. Davis Donates $1 Million to Establish Digital Broadcast Studios At NPF," *National Press Foundation Newsbag.* (December 4, 2013). http://nation-alpress.org/blogs/newsbag/evelyn-y.-davis-donates-1-million-to-establish-digital-broadcast-studios-at/ (accessed 2/26/2014).

37. "Noted Investor and Shareholder Advocate Evelyn Y. Davis Visits the NYSE," *NYSE Euronext NYSE Calendar.* (April 1, 2009). http://www.nyse.com /events/1238494655989.html (accessed 2/26/2014).

38. Dan Duncan. "'Girl Taxi' Service Offers Haven to Beirut's Women," *The Wall Street Journal.* (July 25, 2009). http://online.wsj.com/news/articles /SB124847696096780319 (accessed 2/26/2014).

39. F International Charter, 1984.

40. *Who's Who* (1994). (New York, NY: A.C. Black Publishers, Ltd., St. Martin's Press; "Dame Stephanie (Steve) Shirley, Life President Xansa plc (previously F.I. Group)," *Who's Who 2002.* http://www.mi2g.net/cgi/mi2g/reports/speeches/dss_ profile.pdf (accessed 2/26/2014).

Dr. Diane Franklin with Asst. Prof. Janice McCormick. "F International (A), (B), and (C)," *Harvard Business School Case Studies,* Nos. 9-486-118, -119, -120 and 9-490-004. (Cambridge, MA: Harvard Business School Press, 1986). Dame Steve Shirley's website: http://www.steveshirley.com (accessed 2/26/2014).

41. Computer Developments Ltd. (CDL) was a subsidiary of ICL, England's leading computer manufacturing firm. In 1969, ICL became known as one of the innovators of part-time work at home software development through their own Contract Program Services branch of their systems programming division, which duplicated the F International model. Fujitsu Services began the takeover of ICL in 1990.

42. Eliza G. C. Collins. "A Company without Offices: Steve Shirley Interviewed by Eliza G. C. Collins," *Harvard Business Review* (Cambridge, MA: Harvard Business School Press, January–February 1986), 133.

43. Steria's website: http://www.steria.co.uk (accessed 2/26/2014).

44. In 1997, Tandem Computers was acquired by Compaq Computer Inc. and operated as the NonStop product line. Hewlett-Packard acquired Compaq in 2003. (Tandem was founded in 1974 by four engineers who left HP to build a line of fault tolerant computers.)

45. Oxford Internet Institute's website: http://www.oii.ox.ac.uk (accessed 2/26/2014).

46. Dame Stephanie Shirley with Richard Askwith. *Let It Go: The Story of the Entrepreneur Turned Ardent Philanthropist* (Bedfordshire, UK: Andrews UK Limited, October 29, 2012), website: http://www.let-it-go.co.uk/ (accessed 2/26/2014).

47. Dick Youngblood. "Every Gathering She Plans is an Event," *Star Tribune,* May 18, 2005. http://www.highbeam.com/doc/1G1-132572621.html

48. Haruki Murakami. *Kafka on the Shore* (Knopf; January 18, 2005) 6.

CHAPTER FIVE: IN THE MEDIA

1. Pat Heim, PhD, and Susan A. Murphy, PhD, MBA, with Susan K. Golant. *In the Company of Women: Indirect Aggression among Women; How We Hurt Each Other and How to Stop* (New York, NY: Jeremy P. Tarcher/Putnam, 2003).

2. Carly Fiorina speech at Simmons School of Management 25th Annual Conference. (May 1, 2004). http://www.hp.com/hpinfo/execteam/speeches/fiorina /simmons04.html (accessed 2/26/2014).

3. Carly Fiorina. "The 114th Commencement Address by Carly Fiorina, President and Chief Executive Officer, Hewlett-Packard Company 1999–2005," *North Carolina Agricultural and Technical State University.* (May 7, 2005). http://www.keefamily.org/download/CARLY_FIORINA.pdf (accessed 2/26/2014).

4. Heim/Murphy, 53.

5. Heim/Murphy, 107–115.

6. Heim/Murphy, 21–30.

7. Heim/Murphy, 23.

8. Heim/Murphy, 72.

9. Heim/Murphy, 69–70.

10. Heim/Murphy, 70–71.

11. Heim/Murphy, 24.

12. Heim/Murphy, 26.

13. Heim/Murphy, 60.

14. Heim/Murphy, 26–28.

15. Heim/Murphy, 49.

16. Pauline R. Clance and Suzanne A. Imes. "The Imposter Phenomenon in High Achieving Women: Dynamics and Therapeutic Intervention," *Psychotherapy: Theory, Research & Practice*, 15 no. 3 (Fall 1978), 241–247. http://www.paulineroseclance.com/pdf/ip_high_achieving_women.pdf (accessed 2/26/2014).

17. Clance/Imes, 36.

18. Clance/Imes, 235–241.

19. Clance/Imes, 53.

20. Anna Fels. *Necessary Dreams: Ambition in Women's Changing Lives* (New York, NY: Pantheon, 2004)

21. Anna Fels. "Do Women Lack Ambition?" *Harvard Business Review.* (Cambridge, MA: April 2004). http://ecampus.nmit.ac.nz/moodle/file.php/4599 /Diversity/HBR%20-%20Fels,%20Do%20women%20lack%20ambition,%20 2004.pdf (accessed 2/26/2014).

22. Book Review of *Necessary Dreams, Publishers' Weekly.* (2/16/2004). http://www.publishersweekly.com/978-0-679-44244-8 (accessed 2/26/2014).

23. Fels, 254.

24. Max Ehrmann, "Desiderata" (Terre Haute, IN: 1927).

25. Carol Gallagher, PhD, with Susan K. Golant. *Going to the Top: A Road Map for Success from America's Leading Women Executives, Based on Lessons from 200 Women at the Top of America's Fortune 1000 Companies* (New York, NY: Viking, 2000).

26. Barbara Stanny. *Secrets of Six-Figure Women: Surprising Strategies to Up Your Earnings and Change Your Life* (New York, NY: HarperCollins Publishers, 2002).

27. Stanny, 46.

28. Stanny, 46–47.

29. Evelyn Murphy and E. J. Graffe. *Getting Even: Why Women Don't Get Paid Like Men and What to Do about It* (New York, NY: Touchstone Publishing, 2006).

30. The Wage Project Inc. http://www.wageproject.org (accessed 2/26/2014).

31. Ellen Welty. "Are Your Words Holding You Back?" *Redbook/Hearst Communications Inc.* (March 17, 2005). http://www.redbookmag.com/health-wellness/advice/words-holding-you-back (accessed 2/26/2014).

32. Lois Frankel, PhD. *See Jane Lead: 99 Ways for Women to Take Charge at Work* (New York, NY: Warner Business Books, 2007).

33. Elga Wasserman, PhD. *The Door in the Dream: Conversations with Eminent Women in Science* (Washington, DC: National Academy Press, June 2000).

34. Wasserman, 199.

35. Wasserman, 219.

36. Regents' Lecturer Elga Wasserman. "The Unfinished Agenda—Women in Science and Engineering," *University of California Television* (La Jolla, CA: UCTV, 6/30/2003). http://www.uctv.tv/search-details.aspx?showID=7080 (accessed 2/26/2014).

37. Sky Canaves and Sue Feng. "Hu Shuli's New Magazine Venture," *The Wall Street Journal* (China Real Time, January 7, 2010). http://blogs.wsj.com/chinar-ealtime/2010/01/07/hu-shulis-new-magazine-venture/ (accessed 2/26/2014).

CHAPTER SIX: IN POLITICS

1. Candace Mach. "Getting Personal with Ronna Romney," *Yahoo Contributor News* (June 12, 2012). http://news.yahoo.com/getting-personal-ronna-romney-231100639.html (accessed 2/26/2014).

2. Ronna Romney with Beppie Harrison. *Momentum: Women in American Politics Now* (New York, NY: Crown Publishers Inc., 1988).

3. Romney, 214.

4. "Voting and Registration in the Election of November 2010," U.S. Census. Table 6: Reported Voting and Registration, by Sex, Employment Status, Class of Worker and Disability Status. (November 2010). http://www.census.gov/hhes/www /socdemo/voting/publications/p20/2010/Table6_2010.xls (accessed 2/26/2014).

5. "Fact Sheet: Gender Differences in Voter Turnout," Center for American Women and Politics (CAWP), Eagleton Institute of Politics, Rutgers, the State University of New Jersey (New Brunswick, NJ: 2011). http://www.cawp.rutgers .edu/fast_facts/voters/documents/genderdiff.pdf (accessed 2/26/2014).

6. "Women Mayors in U.S. Cities 2014," CAWP. http://www.cawp.rutgers. edu/fast_facts/levels_of_office/Local-WomenMayors.php (accessed 2/26/2014).

7. "Women in State Legislatures 2014," CAWP. http://www.cawp.rutgers .edu/fast_facts/levels_of_office/documents/stleg.pdf (accessed 2/26/2014).

8. "Women in the U.S. Congress 2014," CAWP. http://www.cawp.rutgers .edu/fast_facts/levels_of_office/documents/cong.pdf (accessed 2/26/2014).

9. "Women in the U.S. Congress 2014," CAWP.

10. "Fact Sheet: History of Women Governors," CAWP. http://www.cawp.rutgers.edu/fast_facts/levels_of_office/documents/govhistory.pdf (accessed 2/26/2014).

11. "Fact Sheet: Women Appointed to Presidential Cabinets," CAWP. http://www.cawp.rutgers.edu/fast_facts/levels_of_office/documents/prescabinet.pdf (accessed 2/26/2014).

12. Robb Mandelbaum. "Meet Maria Contreras-Sweet: An S.B.A. Nominee with Lending Experience," *You're The Boss* blog, *New York Times* (January 17, 2014). http://boss.blogs.nytimes.com/2014/01/17/meet-maria-contreras-sweet-an-s-b-a-nominee-with-lending-experience/ (accessed 2/26/2014).

13. 15 U.S.C.§1691 et seq. http://www.law.cornell.edu/uscode/text/15/1691 (accessed 2/26/2014).

14. Emily W. Card website. http://www.emilycard.net (accessed 2/26/2014); Janice Mall. "Emily Card Continues Credit Crusade," *Los Angeles Times* (May 19, 1985). http://articles.latimes.com/1985-05-19/news/vw-9497_1_credit-card-application (accessed 2/26/2014).

15. Public Law No. 92-318, 86 Stat. 235 (June 23, 1972), codified at 20 U.S.C. sections 1681 through 1688. http://www.law.cornell.edu/uscode/text/20/1681 (accessed 2/26/2014).

16. "Patsy T. Mink" in *Women in Congress, 1917–2006*. Prepared under the direction of the Committee on House Administration by the Office of History & Preservation, U.S. House of Representatives. (Washington, DC: Government Printing Office, 2006). http://bioguide.congress.gov/scripts/biodisplay.pl?index=m000797 (accessed 2/26/2014).

17. Rick Schmitt. "Profit and Loss," *Stanford Alumni News* (March/April 2009). https://alumni.stanford.edu/get/page/magazine/article/?article_id=30885 (accessed 2/26/2014).

18. "CFTC Issues Concept Release Concerning Over-the-Counter Derivatives Market," Release: #4142-98. (May 7, 1998). http://www.cftc.gov/opa/press98/opa4142-98.htm (accessed 2/26/2014).

19. "Over-the-Counter Derivatives Concept Release," Commodity Futures Trading Commission. http://www.cftc.gov/opa/press98/opamntn.htm (accessed 2/26/2014).

20. "Testimony of Brooksley Born, Chairperson, Commodity Futures Trading Commission Concerning the Over-the-Counter Derivatives Market before the U.S. House of Representatives Committee on Banking and Financial Services," (July 24, 1998). http://www.cftc.gov/opa/speeches/opaborn-33.htm (accessed 2/26/2014).

21. "Derivatives Regulation in a High-Tech Age: The Lessons of Long-Term Capital Management, L.P." Remarks of Brooksley Born, Chairperson, Commodity Futures Trading Commission, Conference on Technology in the Marketplace at The Brookings Institute. (October 23, 1998). http://www.cftc.gov/opa/speeches/opaborn-38.htm (accessed 2/26/2014).

22. "Award Recipient Brooksley Born (2009)," John F. Kennedy Presidential Library and Museum. http://www.jfklibrary.org/Events-and-Awards/Profile -in-Courage-Award/Award-Recipients/Brooksley-Born-2009.aspx   (accessed 2/26/2014).

23. Manuel Roig-Franzia. "Brooksley Born, the Cassandra of the Derivatives Crisis," *The Washington Post* (May 26, 2009). http://www.washingtonpost.com/ wp-dyn/content/article/2009/05/25/AR2009052502108.html   (accessed 2/26/2014).

24. John D. McKinnon and Corey Boles. "Panel Set for Probe into Crisis," *The Wall Street Journal* (July 17, 2009). http://online.wsj.com/news/articles /SB124767515048346221 (accessed 2/26/2014).

25. Section 5 of the Fraud Enforcement and Recovery Act of 2009, or FERA, (Pub. Law 111-21, 123 Stat. 1617, S. 386) signed May 20, 2009. http://www.gpo .gov/fdsys/pkg/PLAW-111publ21/content-detail.html (accessed 2/26/2014).

26. Ian Katz. "Brooksley Born Says Too-Big-to-Fail Banks Are Still Economy Risk," *Bloomberg* (April 3, 2013). http://www.bloomberg.com/news/2013-04-03 /brooksley-born-says-too-big-to-fail-banks-are-still-economy-risk.html (accessed 2/26/2014).

27. Sandra Day O'Connor with H. Alan Day. *Lazy B: Growing Up on a Cattle Ranch in the American Southwest* (New York, NY: Random House, 2002).

28. O'Connor, 237–246.

29. O'Connor, quoting R. Lewis Bowman from *Bumfuzzled Too* (R.L. Bowman: 2000), 237.

30. Excerpts from *Lazy B: Growing Up on a Cattle Ranch in the American Southwest* by Sandra Day O'Connor and H. Alan Day, copyright © 2002 by Sandra Day O'Connor and H. Alan Day. Used by permission of Random House, an imprint and division of Random House LLC. All rights reserved.

31. "Presidential Watch: Women Presidential and Vice Presidential Candidates, A Selected List," CAWP. http://www.cawp.rutgers.edu/fast_facts/levels_of_of- fice/documents/prescand.pdf (accessed 2/26/2014).

32. Senator John F. Kennedy. "Would You Want Your Daughter to Be President?" *Everywoman's Magazine*, 6 no. 11. (New York, NY: November 1956), 12. http://planetwaves.net/news/womens-rights/would-you-want-your-daughter- to-be-president/ (accessed 2/26/2014).

CHAPTER SEVEN: IN MEMORIAM

1. Jocelyn Y. Stewart. "Ad Executive Broke Barriers for Women," *Los Angeles Times*, Obituary. February 8, 2008. http://articles.latimes.com/2008/feb/08/local /me-hall8 (accessed 2/26/2014).

2. Staff Writers. "Pastor's Wife Co-founded Guideposts," *Los Angeles Times*, Obituary, February 8, 2008. http://articles.latimes.com/2008/feb/08/local/me- peale8 (accessed 2/26/2014).

3. Harriet B. Braiker, PhD, *The Type E Woman: How to Overcome the Stress of Being Everything to Everybody* (New York, NY: Dodd Mead & Co., August 1986).

4. Myrna Oliver. "Harriet B. Braiker, 55; Author Was an Expert on Stress Management," *Los Angeles Times*, Obituary January 13, 2004. http://www.diseasetoplease.com/obituary.htm (accessed 2/26/2014).

5. Braiker, *Type E Woman*, 213.

6. Braiker, 209.

7. Braiker, 213 ff.

8. Caroline Fairchild. "Women CEOs in the Fortune 1000: By the Numbers." Fortune magazine. July 8, 2014. http://fortune.com/2014/07/08/women-ceos-fortune-500-1000/retrieved 7/21/2014.

9. "First Woman on a Corporate Board," Virtual Chase Archive, copyright 2008 by Ballard Spahr Andrews & Ingersoll, LLP (now Ballard Spahr LLP). http://archive.virtualchase.justia.com/ask_answer/first_woman.html (accessed 2/26/2014)..

10. "Administration Building to Be Named for Lettie Pate Whitehead Evans." http://gtalumni.org/Publications/techtopics/sum98/black.html (accessed 2/26/2014).

11. The Lettie Pate Whitehead Foundation website: http://www.lpwhitehead.org/ (accessed 2/26/2014).

12. The Lettie Pate Evans Foundation website: http://www.lpevans.org/ (accessed 2/26/2014).

13. Kenneth Lisenbee. "Marjorie Merriweather Post: A Biography." http://www.paulbowles.org/marjoriemerriweatherpost.html (accessed 2/26/2014).

14. Hillwood Estate, Museum & Gardens. http://www.hillwoodmuseum.org/about-hillwood (accessed 2/26/2014).

15. "Barbara Ringer, 1973–1980; Acting, 1993–1994," U.S. Copyright Office. http://www.copyright.gov/history/bios/ringer/ringer.html (accessed 2/26/2014).

16. Matt Schudel. "Barbara Ringer, 83; Crafted Updating of Copyright Law," *The Washington Post. The Boston Globe*, Obituary. April 27, 2009 from Boston.com /BostonGlobe. http://www.boston.com/bostonglobe/obituaries/articles/2009/04/27/barbara_ringer_83_crafted_updating_of_copyright_law/ (accessed 2/26/2014).

17. "The Barbara A. Ringer Copyright Honors Program," U.S. Copyright Office. http://www.copyright.gov/careers/career-ringer.html (accessed 2/26/2014).

18. Museum Collections, Maggie L. Walker, National Historic Site, Museum Management Program, U.S. National Park Service, U.S. Department of the Interior. http://www.nps.gov/history/museum/exhibits/Maggie_Walker/index.html (accessed 2/26/2014).

19. Michael Schwartz. "Bank's Heritage Consolidated into the History Books," *Richmond BizSense*, September 2, 2010. http://www.richmondbizsense.com/2010/09/02/banks-heritage-consolidated-into-the-history-books/ (accessed 2/26/2014).

20. "Muriel Siebert—The First Woman of Finance," Muriel Siebert & Co., https://www.siebertnet.com/html/StartAboutMickie.aspx (accessed 2/26/2014).

21. Siebert Financial Corp., 2012 Proxy Statement. https://www.siebertnet.com/documents/PRX2012.pdf (accessed 2/26/2014).

22. "Risk/Reward: Tales of Women on Wall Street." (2003). http://www.imdb.com/title/tt0358079/ (accessed 2/26/2014).

23. March 28, 2008: video clip. http://www.nbcnews.com/video/nightly-news/52849303#52849303 (accessed 2/26/2014). Learn Money, presented by the Muriel F. Siebert Foundation Inc. http://www.learnmoney.org/about-us (accessed 7/26/2014).

24. "Elinor Ostrom, Indiana University Faculty Member, Wins Nobel Prize for Economics." Indiana University News Room, October 12, 2009. http://newsinfo.iu.edu/news/page/normal/12185.html (accessed 2/26/2014).

25. Ibid.

26. Elinor Ostrom (1933–2012) Curriculum Vitae. http://www.indiana.edu/~workshop/people/lostromcv.htm (accessed 2/26/2014).

27. Elinor Ostrom. *Understanding Institutional Diversity* (Princeton, NJ: Princeton University Press, 2005).

28. Peter Boettke. George Mason University, book review at Princeton University Press. http://press.princeton.edu/titles/8085.html (accessed 2/26/2014).

29. Elinor Ostrom. *Governing the Commons: The Evolution of Institutions for Collective Action* (Political Economy of Institutions and Decisions) (Cambridge, UK: Cambridge University Press, November 30, 1990).

30. Book review from *Contemporary Sociology: A Journal of Reviews* (Washington, DC: American Sociological Association, November 1990). http://www.cambridge.org/us/academic/subjects/politics-international-relations/political-economy/governing-commons-evolution-institutions-collective-action (accessed 2/26/2014).

About the Author

Elizabeth Ghaffari is the founder, president, and CEO of Technology Place Inc., a California-based company that provides technical consulting services for business clients in need of successful e-business strategies and enhanced electronic communications with customers and business partners.

She established Champion Boards as a service of Technology Place Inc. to foster the design of great boards of directors through knowledge and information, with a special emphasis on the advancement of top-level women to corporate board roles. She is the author of *Outstanding in Their Field: How Women Corporate Directors Succeed* (Praeger, 2009) and *Women Leaders at Work: Untold Tales of Women Achieving Their Ambitions* (Apress: 2011).

Ghaffari earned her master's degree in management from the Anderson School of Business, University of California at Los Angeles, and her bachelor of arts degree in political science from The American University in Washington, DC. She attended the Inaugural Corporate Governance Program at Stanford University Graduate School of Business, Executive Education Program.